Enter at A, Laughing

Enter at A, Laughing
By
Brian McKeown

A Tongue-in-Jowl Examination of the Sport of Dressage
as seen through
the Satirical Eyes of a Dressage Husband.

Those that can, ride. Those that can't, write.

> **Warning:**
> *All of the information contained
> in this book is totally unreliable.*

Half Halt Press, Inc.
Boonsboro, Maryland

Enter at A, Laughing: A Tongue-in-Jowl Examination of the Sport of Dressage as seen through the Satirical Eyes of a Dressage Husband

©2003 Brian McKeown

Published in the United States of America by
Half Halt Press, Inc.
P.O. Box 67
Boonsboro, MD 21713

Illustrations by Jim Haynes, Grapics Plus
Front and back cover photos by Carole McDonald

isbn 0-939481-64-2

Library of Congress Cataloging-in-Publication Data

McKeown, Brian.
    Enter at A, laughing: a tongue-in-jowl examination of the sport of
dressage as seen through the satirical eyes of a dressage husband
/ by Brian McKeown; [illustrations by Jim Haynes].
        p. cm.
    "Those that can, ride. Those that can't, write."
    ISBN 0-939481-65-0
    1. Horsemanship--Humor. 2. Dressage--Humor. I. Title.

SF301.M47 2003
798.2'3--dc21

                                                                2003050824

To Sue,
My Sweetheart

ACKNOWLEDGEMENTS

I take most of the responsibility for the silliness contained in this book, but there are plenty of other folk who must shoulder their share of the blame. A major culprit is Elizabeth Carnes of Half Halt Press who, in a tragic moment of weakness, put her reputation on the line and agreed to publish this heap of nonsense. Thank you, Beth.

Next, I am grateful to the following members of several writers groups for their invaluable feedback, normally responsible and rational people who should have known better: Joan Cass, Liz West, Carlene Philips, Ron Bachman, Rachel Alexander-Hill, Dan Gordon, Barbara McCullough, Bonnie Cameron, and especially Betsy Gitelman and Larry Kessinich.

I would also like to thank several dressage friends who provided support and who have asked to remain anonymous. They are Heidi Scholes, Irene Greenberg, Ellen Zanino, Patricia Lasko of *Dressage Today* and Treva Tucker. Many thanks also to Priscilla Endicott, Kathy Connelly, Julie Alnwick and the Board of the New England Dressage Association for allowing me to take their names in vain. At least, I'm sure that they would have allowed me if I had asked them. Plus I want to thank Jim Hayes for drawing the cartoons and Carole MacDonald for taking the pictures. I don't want to forget to thank our two horses, Gus and Marty, plus my dog Gromit, who provided me with inspiration just by being there.

Finally, I am deeply grateful to my wonderful wife Sue, who had the idea for a dressage humor book in the first place. Without her help, ideas and encouragement, this project would never have been completed and I would still be shoveling horse manure. Come to think of it, I *am* still shoveling horse manure.

Table of Contents

INTRODUCTION 11

CONFESSIONS OF A DRESSAGE HUSBAND 16
The things you do for love

SNIPPETS OF DRESSAGE HISTORY: 21
LADY GODIVA REVEALS ALL
Medieval dressage queen *barely* finishes test

U.S. TEAM SIFTS OUT BRONZE MEDAL 24
AT MUCKERS COMPETITION
Fame at last for those that clean stalls

A WORD ABOUT THE JUDGES 31
God bless 'em, one and all

ASK MR. DRESSAGE HUSBAND 33
Burning questions answered for dressage widowers

SNIPPETS OF DRESSAGE HISTORY: 39
THE ORIGINS OF PRIX ST. GEORGES
Straight from the warmblood's mouth

COMMON DRESSAGE AILMENTS 41
It only hurts when you ride

ARE HORSES SMARTER THAN MEN? 47
A rhetorical question examined

SNIPPETS OF DRESSAGE HISTORY: 52
PAUL REVERE'S BIG NIGHT OUT
The 'true' origin of the dressage ring letters

CREATIVE MANURE MANAGEMENT 57
Yankee ingenuity at its best

ADVANCED CLICKER CLINIC FOR DRESSAGE HUSBANDS 63
Improving your relationship without words

A FAUX PAS AT NEDA FALL 69
Helping the judges with their comments

SNIPPETS ETC, ETC, ETC: 72
THE ORIGINS OF PIAFFE
The truth at last, mon ami

HOME IS WHERE THE HORSE IS 75
Whole lotta shakin' in Harvard Yard

FANCY FRENCH PHRASOLOGY 81
How to parlez-vous avec les crème de la crème

PASSING THE TIME AT A DRESSAGE SHOW 86
The devil makes work for idle hands

SNIPPETS, WHATEVER: 91
A HORSE, A HORSE, MY KINGDOM FOR A FEI HORSE
Richard III reins in, and reigns no more.

PECULIARITIES OF THE SPORT 97
Curiouser and curiouser

THE TEN COMMANDMENTS OF DRESSAGE 104
Holy Moses, follows these rules religiously

THE HAT IN THE RING: A LOVE STORY 106
A dressage princess and a stable boy proceed at the trot

SNIPPETS BLAH, BLAH, BLAH: DICK TURPIN'S LAST RIDE 118
A highwayman blows away the competition

RIDING TO PERFECTION 123
Tips and techniques from an expert

THE GROMIT TEST 133
How to sneak into heaven through the back door

UFO LANDS IN A DRESSAGE RING 137
Spooks the hell out of everyone

SNIPPETS AND SO ON:
THE EXTENDED TROT OF THE LIGHT BRIGADE 142
A dressage test turns ugly during the Crimean War

I MARRIED A DRESSAGE SHOW SECRETARY 145
And lived to tell the tale

KNOW YOUR HORSE'S ANATOMY 152
A primer for dressage husbands on horse guts

SNIPPETS YADA, YADA, YADA:
FRANCOIS BAUCHER MAKES UP HIS MIND 157
A dressage master sees the light

DRESSAGE MAFIA STRIKES AGAIN 161
Sinister goings-on from dressage hooligans

THIS JUST IN: TIDBITS OF DRESSAGE NEWS 166
The latest info from the crazy world of dressage

SNIPPETS AD NAUSEAM:
DRESSAGE COMPETITION DURING THE TROJAN WAR 171
The Trojan Horse—myth or reality show?

CLASSIFIEDS ADS 178
What you need, going cheap

Introduction

This book consists of a collection of articles and essays of satirical, tongue-in-jowl, semi-humorous dressage-related fun. You may have noticed that there does not appear to be many humor books that deal specifically with this particular equestrian discipline, so I think it's safe to assume that dressage humor books are as rare as scoring a ten on a canter pirouette. Why is that, you might ask?

Well, one reason is that trying to find humor in the sport of dressage is like trying to find humor in a kidney transplant. Dressage is an intensely serious and elite equestrian endeavor in which frivolity plays no part. It concerns itself with the spiritual and physical quest of realizing perfect harmony between horse and rider. There is nothing even remotely amusing about that now, is there? So you might be wondering why someone would be crazy enough to attempt to write an entire book of dressage humor, particularly someone who was once described by an editor of a dressage magazine as "knowing just enough about dressage to be dangerous. Well, it's a long story, but I'm going to tell it to you anyway.

It began one drizzly morning a couple of years ago when I was mucking out the stalls of my wife's two horses, listening to a Gilbert and Sullivan operetta on the CD player. (I was listening to Gilbert and Sullivan, not the horses. They are Swedish, so naturally Gilbert and Sullivan is way beyond their sensitivities). And it occurred to me that, like the operetta, my life had become a happy little farce. My thirty-year career in the computer industry was over (thank heavens, because I never understood the damn things anyway). As an early retirement volunteer, I was sitting pretty at last. No more stress, no more tension—now I'm a simple house husband and horse minder. I thought, how hard can that be?

But it turned out to be a somewhat hollow existence. As intellectually stimulating as shoveling horse manure is, and as blindingly exciting as pulling around a vacuum cleaner can be, I needed another creative outlet. So I decided to write humorous articles about dressage from the point of view of a dressage husband, thereby saving myself a great deal of money on therapy sessions. Initially I was aware that my writing needed some improvement, as the syntax was poor, the grammar was stilted, the pace was uneven, the structure was atrocious and the content was sophomoric. Otherwise, it was close to perfection. So, when several of my articles were published in the New England Dressage Association's publications, *The Tip of the Hat* and *The Salute*, it became clear to everyone that the publishers needed to change their medication. Thankfully, the New England dressage community are such sophisticated, light-hearted folks that they didn't mind me poking a little fun at them in their own magazines, and would often approach me at dressage shows to pelt me with manure. Then my wife, Sue, suggested that I should write an entire collection of dressage humor pieces and get the whole load of nonsense out of my system once and for all. It's collaborative support such as that which makes our relationship so special, plus of course our personalities totally complement each other, she being an Adult Amateur and I being an Amateur Adult.

You will notice that throughout this book I have strove, strived, striven to be politically incorrect, deliberately biasing all gender-related references to the feminine side of the human species. So I say "her" to mean "her" *and* "him;" I say women to mean women *and* men. I don't say he or she; I say she to mean both. It's about bloody time, don't you think? I am aware that fifteen percent or so of dressage riders are male, but frankly I've marginalized them. My experience of male dressage riders tells me they can handle it. Since the invention of the written word, before Socrates was sucking eggs, literature has always pushed women to the back of the chariot, bundling them into the collective male genre, like so much clutter. In the sport of dressage women are the large majority, so any male participants are just going to have to accept the prejudice that women have had to endure since Moses pulled out those gender-biased commandments from under his sackcloth—at least in this book. Still, both you and I know that the male ego is nothing to be trifled with, so, by way of compensation, I refer to all horses as male—with apologies to you mare owners.

In addition, I have avoided the word "equestrienne" because it sounds prissy and patronizing. And I refer to equestrian expertise throughout as horsepersonship, not necessarily to be politically correct, but mainly because I enjoy being a smartass.

Since we have already established that dressage humor is an oxymoron, trying to dig up a few chuckles on the subject is a difficult assignment. Nevertheless, being a person of refinement, I've tried to ensure that I didn't stoop to using those two old standbys of the stand-up comic in trouble, i.e. sex and the toilet. I tried, but I failed miserably. So you will find lots of sexual innuendo and probably too many references to manure spread throughout these pages. I'm telling you this so you won't think that I am obsessed with sex and manure. Sex maybe—but definitely not manure. Okay, okay, manure too.

Another easy target that I've used for cheap laughs is to poke fun at national characteristics. In order not to appear discriminatory, I have strove, strived, striven to ridicule all of the major dressage nations, including England, my birth country, and the United States, my adopted country. I have, however, paid particular attention to Germany and France. Why? Well, because I'm British, so I couldn't help it. I apologize if I have omitted a country for which you have a particular affinity—I'll try and ridicule it in any future publications.

On a more serious note, you will find splattered throughout this book several articles entitled *Snippets of Dressage History* of which I am particularly fond. Since a few of these articles have appeared in dressage magazines, several astute, yet constipated, historians have been quick to point out that these snippets bear little relation to the historical facts. Such unfounded criticism is… well, unfounded. I have spent buckets of time meticulously researching each article to ensure total accuracy. For example, I spent almost the entire afternoon last Tuesday reading up on the Wars of the Roses for the Richard III snippet. I even went out and bought the Cliffs Notes. So when I am subjected to ridicule from so-called "experts," simply because they have some fancy doctorate or other on some totally obscure historical subject, it really frosts my britches. Sure, I may have stretched the occasional historical truth and, sure, many of these snippets have little basis in reality, but I invoke my right to use "humorist license" (which is similar to "poetic license," except you don't have to get the stuff to rhyme).

One final word. To my brother dressage husbands out there, to those unappreciated, wonderfully supportive spouses, playing second fiddle as they do to a huge ugly lump of sweating horse flesh, I say this: if you get as much fun out of reading this book as I did in writing it, then my mission is accomplished.

Confessions of a Dressage Husband
The things you do for love

To be honest, for most of my life I never really gave horses much thought. If pressed for an opinion I probably would have subscribed to the "uncomfortable in the middle, dangerous at both ends" school of thought. Then I had the good fortune to meet and marry Sue, a Dressage Queen of the first order, who loves riding the beasts with a passion. I will always remember when, during our wedding ceremony, she whispered in my ear how she felt so happy that she had found such a wonderful groom. At that point, I had no idea that the difference between her definition of the word *groom* and mine would have such a profound effect on my future. That was fifteen years ago and, since then, my life has been, somewhat reluctantly, horse intensive, although horse infested may be a more accurate description. I became that pathetic of all inconsequential spouses, a "dressage husband."

Now, I'm not one to complain. My wife's obsession with these obtuse animals, I rationalized, was a small price to pay for the unremitting joys that marriage to her would sooner or later evoke. Being the sensitive, Renaissance male that I am, I decided to support her equine endeavors in whatever form they might take, and at whatever emotional or financial cost. If she was happy, I figured, then I would be happy or, at least, get some peace and quiet. Of course, little did I realize that owning and showing dressage horses costs about as much as the Gross National Product of most Central American countries. This financial burden became starkly obvious when I learned that both of her horses would lovingly receive two pair of very expensive new shoes every six weeks, while I would be lucky to get a pair of Reeboks every two years. Nevertheless, I attended all of the dressage shows in which she competed to provide her with sympathetic moral support, and to clean her boots before she entered the ring.

I even pretended that I understood the intricacies of this incredibly obscure sport. "That transition was somewhat parochial, wouldn't you say, but still lucid," I would remark to the nearest fellow spectator. "Pity that lethargic impulsion besmirched the cohesion of her canter pirouette," I would interject into any huddle of dressage experts, with the confidence of knowing that I had no idea what I was talking about. Mind you, I found that I enjoyed the company of horse people. Intelligent, self-assured women, who own more than their share of leather and whips, are just fine in my estimation.

Early in our relationship, Sue shared her dearest dream with me. She wanted her own barn, where she could pamper her two horsies like royal children. My dream was to retire early—after all I had been working since I was fif-

teen—so I could pursue my own hobby of taking a nap. Then, several years ago, by dint of hard work and a little bit of luck, our dreams came true. We bought a house on a gentle hill. At the bottom of the hill, we had a small but elegant barn constructed, with standing paddocks leading to larger paddocks, and a full size dressage ring, accurately marked out with those letters that nobody really understands. The barn was replete with features to ensure a horse heaven, and Sue could sit out on the patio in the evening, Chardonnay in hand, and look down on her beloved animals idyllically munching away in their well-tended paddocks. Sue was in heaven.

I also realized my dream. The company that had employed me for 26 years was gobbled up by a more successful company, and I took advantage of the early retirement plan. Immediately, I went out and bought a leather couch, perfect for a good after-lunch snooze. The fly in the ointment of my new found happiness, however, was that I had to take care of the horses while my wife was at work. This meant that I had to muck out the stalls.

Muck is an appropriate word for this type of endeavor, although stronger words come to mind. Nevertheless, I attacked the task with wholehearted gusto until, it was frightening to discover, I was actually good at it. The skill, I learned, was in sifting the manure from the shavings. Not the smallest piece of horse feces could hide from my expert technique. I perfected the over-the-shoulder flick into the wheelbarrow, without the use of any Annie Oakley-style mirror. An immaculate manure-free stall became a matter of pride. When I would run into old colleagues who would ask me what I was doing now that I had retired, I would respond with, "More or less the same thing that I was doing before I retired."

On a trip to England last Christmas, I was handed an immigration form by the flight attendant, which asked for my occupation. Embarrassed to answer "Professional Couch Potato," I wrote down, "Equine Waste Disposal Consultant," which seemed to impress the customs official to no end. And while in England I discovered and purchased a technologically advanced, state-of-the-art horse pooper-scooper, which unfortunately aroused the anger of my fellow passengers when I tried to stuff it into the overhead bin on my return flight.

Given my newfound skills, I have petitioned the United States Dressage Federation to include a competition for manure sifters at future dressage shows. The riders prance their stuff in the ring and are rewarded with accolades and ribbons, but who gives a thought for the poor peons that muck out the stalls? I suggest that a special competition be held at each show for the mucker-outers. Each mucker would have thirty minutes to clean a stall, watched intensely by a judge (three judges for FEI level) who would mark appropriately for technique, speed and thoroughness, making professional comments to a scribe. Any equine fecal pieces left larger than 30cm would require an automatic one-point deduction. The marks would be rushed via runners to the scorers who would post them proudly on the scoreboard. The winning mucker would be required to trot a lap of honor around the ring holding aloft the winning mucking fork to which the blue ribbon would be attached.

So what do you think? Good idea? Send your supportive comments to your local dressage association and let the groundswell begin.

Snippets of Dressage History # XXIX:
Lady Godiva reveals all

Even in equestrian circles, it is little known that Lady Godiva was one of history's first dressage champions. Lady Godiva, a woman of indisputable beauty and ineffable grace, is renown for having ridden through the streets of Coventry, England, naked as a jaybird, some time between the late dark ages and the early middle ages.

The whole episode began during a tiff between the Lady and her husband, Lord Godiva, well known tyrant and chocolate magnate. His Lordship complained to his wife that she was spending way too much money and attention on her passion for dressage. In those far off days dressage husbands had not yet accepted what we today take for granted: poverty and loneliness are small prices to pay for marriage to a dressage queen. As their argument reached its climax, His Lordship, in a fiery temper, declared that his wife would have to ride buck-naked through the city before he would pay for one more damn shadbelly, horse brush or equine acupuncture session. Being a closet exhibitionist,

Lady Godiva could not have been more pleased at this suggestion and the rest, as they say, is history.

Her Ladyship owned a stable full of first-rate FEI dressage horses, and naturally she chose a warmblood for her famous ride, on the rationale that her tushy would be better protected from the cold Coventry wind. The whole event was a big hit, particularly with the men of the town and Lord Godiva found, as an added bonus, that he enjoyed a new respect from his male serfs. The judges were also male, which accounts for why Lady Godiva's famous ride was the only dressage test in history to score a perfect ten for every movement.

To celebrate this historic event, the winners of all dressage competitions in the middle ages were required thereafter to ride a victory gallop in the nude at the end of the event. Many historians believe that this accounts for why dressage was the second most popular medieval spectator sport, next only to the 'Burning of Heretics.' The practice of the nude victory gallop was unfortunately discontinued during the Reformation, confirming the belief that early Lutherans were not a lot of fun.

At a recent United States Dressage Federation board meeting, it was suggested that we resurrect this long lost dressage tradition for future competitions, but the motion was narrowly defeated by a vote of 24 to one. Nevertheless, you would do well to remember the vital contribution that Lady Godiva and her courageous ride made to popularizing the great sport of dressage—next time that you take a shower.

U.S. Team Sifts Bronze at Third Annual Muckers Competition
Fame at last for those that clean stalls

In my earlier article, Confessions of a Dressage Husband, I advocated that a competition be established to recognize the efforts and expertise for those who clean stalls. Little did I know that such a competition already existed and at an international level no less. So I was delighted to attend when the competition was held here in the United States and was able to file the following report.

Brian McKeown
Show Correspondent

As rank outsiders, the members of the United States Team were delighted to capture the Bronze Medal at the Third Annual International Muckers Competition held last week at the Love Canal Farm in Upstate New York. The first time that the competition has been held in the United States, event organizer Wendi Problowski was pleased to report that the entire three day procedure went off extremely smoothly, with a record 16 equestrian nations taking part.

"Unlike the first two International Competitions there was surprisingly little bloodshed, and the police only had to be called three times," Wendi stated, with justifiable pride. "The biggest disappointment," Wendi continued, "was the extraordinary number of national teams that were disqualified; a clear indication that we need to be more explicit on rule definition if we want to avoid this problem in future competitions."

Sponsored by the United States Dressage Federation, the Muckers Competition celebrates the skills of the usually forgotten peons that muck out horse stalls every day—every stinking day—of the year. These gallant and under-appreciated, not to mention underpaid, horse lovers, crouching as they do at the bottom of the social equestrian ladder, perform such essential tasks that the equestrian community could not function without them. Usually referred to as "Muckers," but are also sometimes called "Sifters" or "Those People," they have received little public recognition until recently.

The first international competition to honor their contribution was held in Sainte Loo, France—a country no stranger to the shoveling of excrement, and where the competition was originally titled, "Le Merde au Cheval Internationale." Last year the competition was held in Montevideo, Uruguay, where the Brazilian team triumphed. Unfortunately, the closing ceremonies were marred when the Brazilians set off firecrackers causing a major fire in the main barn. By dint of sheer luck and some individual heroics, no horses were injured in the conflagration, (although it is believed that maybe a few of the Muckers perished). Animal psychologists were brought in to help ensure that the affected horses would not suffer any long-term mental problems.

This year's competition included a Freestyle event, in addition to the usual Individual and Team Championship. Muckers are required to clean out a horse stall, put down fresh shavings, clean out the feed and the water buckets, kill any flies in the stall, push a wheelbarrow full of horse manure fifty yards to a manure pile, empty it, then race back to the start line—all within 20 minutes. Points are awarded for style, presentation and panache. Points are deducted for time overrun, cursing, pouting and any horse feces left in the stall greater than ten centimeters in diameter. Three judges are used at the international level, and the stalls used in the competition had been occupied by a herd of Clydesdales, who have been fed a double ration of bran mash the night before.

"The quality of the competition at this year's event was exceptional," explained Wendi. "Even though the competitive spirit was intense between the individual nations, competitors from different national cultures seem to coexist tied by a common bond—a love of the smell of horse stalls in the morning that transcends all human boundaries."

The Individual Gold Medal winner was the unbeaten German Champion Kraut Von Sauerbrauten, whose legendary precision in sifting every piece, every tiny inconsequential piece of manure, every minute, microscopic, molecule of equine feces is... well, is legendary. The German team however, did not fare as well. Odds-on favorites to win the event, the Germans found themselves in a shouting match with the French team, exchanging insults just two stalls away. Pretty soon the two antagonists began lobbing horse turds at each other until the furious Germans, brushing aside the Belgian team competing in the stall that separated them from the French, hurled themselves onto their Gallic neighbors. "Not exactly an historical precedent—the Germans scrambling over the Belgians to get to the French—if you catch my drift," commented the Belgian captain, Hercule Parrot. The ensuing melee resulted in the arrest of the entire German team, whose cause was not helped by their use of titanium-tipped mucking forks that added a new dimension to the term "body piercing" when applied to the French injuries. Arraignment is scheduled for next week.

Unfortunately, the Germans were only the first of several teams to suffer disqualification. The Irish were also asked to withdraw from the competition when the urine samples of all of their team members tested positive, with enough Bute in their systems to kill an adult male hippopotamus. The Canadians then became favorites, but they too suffered the same fate, when it was learned that all four Canadian team members were in fact illegal immigrants from Guatemala. Righteous indignation rippled through the spectators, and as one horse lover from Arizona noted, "Using illegal immigrants to muck out horse stalls is abhorrent to us in the United States and would never be tolerated."

The British team fared even worse. Losing their way on leaving Buffalo Airport, they arrived two days after the event was over. The British Team captain, Penelope

Frogbottom-Smythe, giggled, "We all felt so frightfully silly, as we seem to get lost all the bloody time. Still, those State Troopers were ever so polite when they found us driving on the wrong side of the New York State Thruway." Event organizers hadn't the heart to tell the British team that, even if they had arrived on time, they wouldn't have been allowed through the gate let alone compete. Explained Wendi, "What with Hoof and Mouth, Swine Fever, Mad Cow disease, Smallpox, Beri-Beri and Mono that are currently ravaging the Sceptered Isle, I'm surprised the limeys were allowed in the country."

Two other teams scheduled to compete also got lost in transit. The Cuban team finally surfaced at the INS offices in North Tonawanda, NY, demanding political asylum. The Mexican team, however, completely disappeared after landing at La Guardia. "We believe that they must have been so homesick for their country," said Wendy, "that they turned around and headed right back to Mexico."

With all the cancellations, the French team was clearly in the lead by the second day, with the Dutch team close on their heels. The Dutch however lost precious points when their team member, Willem deGouda, suffered an unfortunate accident. As he was racing down a slight incline pushing a fully laden wheelbarrow towards the manure heap, he lost control of the barrow, which then plummeted into the parking lot and smashed into the side of the President of Judges' new Lexus GS 450. It was at this juncture, some onlookers believe, that the objectivity of the judging staff may have become compromised.

So the French team appeared to have the competition wrapped up when, to the amazement of the seven-

member audience, the entire French contingent stormed off in a fit of Gallic pique when their team captain, Suzette Crepe, received less than a perfect ten from the Slovenian judge.

When the smoke cleared, it was the Belgian team, affectionately nicknamed, "The Brussels Sprouts," that was awarded the blue ribbon. Second place went to the team from Mozambique, affectionately known as "the team from Mozambique." Suprisingly, the U.S. grabbed third place, with a team of young stable girls from California: Kelli, Trixi, Trudi and Lawanda. "It was totally awesome, so really, really cool, you know—you know so way out there, you know," spurted Kelli, "We never expected to medal amongst all these really cool European types—you know."

The last day featured the grand finale of the competition—the Freestyle, or better known as "Mucking to Music." The blue ribbon went to the Italian Luigi Boyardee, sifting with elan to a haunting rendition of Vermicelli's Excreta Opus. A close second was the Swede Olaf Smorgasbord, who performed to a medley of really boring

ABBA hits. Third place, again, went to an American, Bettie "Alabama" Grits, who was sifting to the country classic by Billy Bob Outhouse, "How Can I Miss You When You Won't Go Away."

"A wonderfully successful competition," summed up Wendi. "Our sponsors, Charmin Toilet Tissue and Tidybowl, thankfully provided the bail money for the German and the British teams, so all worked out well in the end. Now we all look forward to next year's competition scheduled to be held in Sarajevo, Bosnia."

A Word about the Judges
God bless 'em, one and all

I feel no compunction about poking a little fun at any aspect of the sport of dressage, after all this is a dressage humor book, and my experience with dressage folks is that they take it all in good spirit. I make an exception, however, when it comes to the judges because of the respect I hold for them.

It's clear that dressage judges are the heart of this sport, because not only do they judge the horse's and rider's abilities, a difficult enough task, they also instruct the riders on what needs to be done to improve their skills, on every single move the rider makes. No other sport does that. Dressage judges see their primary role as enhancing the quality of the sport, not simply assessing the ride, and they do this for the love of the sport—they are paid little more than expenses.

Another admirable aspect of all dressage judging is its consistency. The judges are so experienced in the requirements of the various levels of ability that their marks are almost always consistent in their assessment of the same ride.

My wife maintains that when she halts and salutes at X, the people that she salutes deserve the deference.

My wife's name incidentally is Sue, Sue McKeown. She will be riding a beautiful black Swedish Warmblood gelding at Prix St. Georges and Intermediare 1 this year. Her horse's name is Marshal, that's M-A-R-S-H-A-L, and look out for his magnificent extended trot.

Ask Mr. Dressage Husband

Burning questions answered for dressage widowers

Since I began writing horse-related articles from the dressage widower's point of view, I have been inundated by queries from other guys of the same sorry ilk who are baffled by the complexities of the sport. Okay, maybe inundated is too strong a word, but I have received many questions—well perhaps not many, but some at least. A few, just a few, okay (are you satisfied now—now that you've embarrassed me right here in my own article). So as a service to all those pathetic, lonely, penniless husbands and fathers struggling, like the sensitive males that we are, to support our dressage type loved ones by understanding the intricacies of the sport, I humbly present "Ask Mr. Dressage Husband."

Q.   My wife informs me that she needs to purchase a new dressage horse because her current horse lacks "tractability." What does this mean?

                                        — *Confused in Cincinnati*

A. Dear *Confused*:

"Tractability" means that her horse is not strong enough. Back in the days of the early settlers, when women were women and men wore the britches, John Deere invented his famous farm machinery before the discovery of gasoline. So the only way those early tractors would work were for horses to pull them. Hence the measure of a horse's strength became known as its "tractability", that is, how far he could pull a tractor.

Q. **My wife inadvertently left a vial of her horse's urine on the kitchen counter. As the vial was labeled "Coggins," I naturally assumed it was a single malt Scotch, so I mixed it with caffeine-free ginger ale and drank the lot. My question is should I see a doctor or a vet?**

— Legless in Lexington

A. Dear *Legless*:

Mistaking horse urine for alcohol is a common occurrence in dressage households and has formed the basis for a couple of famous and vindictive divorce suits. My advice is not to worry about it. An animal has already processed the liquid so it should pass right through you. Just lay off the bran flakes for a couple of days.

Q. **Why is a horse lover often called a *Hippophile*, and does it refer to all equestrians or only those who are really fat?**

—Stymied in Segunda

A.   Listen, *Stymied:*

This is my column so I'll make the jokes around here. Okay? If you want to know the origin of the word *Hippophile*, you need to go way back to the golden age of ancient Greece, circa 500 BC. The ancient Greek word for horse is *Hippo* (really), and their ancient word for wacko is *phile* (not really). When the ancient Greeks explored Africa, they came across an animal they called Hippopotamus, meaning "water horse" (really). Now I'm aware that those ancient Greeks were supposed to be pretty smart, after all they invented Western civilization in, like, an afternoon. But how in Hades could they have mistaken a hippopotamus for a horse in the water? I could understand them mistaking a zebra for a horse, or even mistaking an antelope for a horse if it was dark and they had bad eye sight. But a hippopotamus? It seems those clever

Greeks may have been smoking a little bit too much hemlock. Imagine what happened when they tried to put a saddle on one, or a bit in his mouth. Mind you, it might be no coincidence that water polo was invented around the same time.

Q.   **My wife occasionally says that she has to go and clean her horse's sheath. What does that mean?**
                                                                — *Clueless in Cleveland*

A.   Dear *Clueless*:
       You don't want to know.

Q.   **It seems that every day a new bill comes in for some type of horse expense. Yesterday, it was for new winter blankets. When I asked my wife if these blankets are necessary, she replied, as expected, that of course they were, although the old blankets look fine to me. If this continues then I'll be bankrupt in no time. Can you please give me some advice?**
                                                                — *Desperate in Detroit*

A.   Dear *Desperate*:
       For heaven's sake, man, quit whining. So your wife wants a few extra bucks to buy some new blankets? Big deal! Do you want her horse to go on wearing old blankets until they are threadbare? How cruel is that? Do you want her horse to be the laughing stock of the barn in his outmoded apparel? Just what kind of selfish, self-absorbed, inconsiderate

husband are you anyway? Consider the stress that your wife is under. She has to worry about the welfare of her horse, she has to ensure that she absorbs and applies all of her trainer's instructions, she has to enter at A, halt at X, and then perform complicated equine maneuvers under the critical eyes of experts. Talk about tension. The last thing she needs to worry about is you carping about money, so my advice is pay-up and be thankful you are blessed with such a woman.

Q.   **I overheard her trainer tell my daughter during a training session that "the flexion of the poll should remain unaltered." I've never heard of this expression before. What does it mean?**
— Perplexed in Pittsburgh

A.   Dear *Perplexed*:
I have no idea.

Q.   **Can a dressage horse hear and react to Freestyle music? Is it actually moving to the music?**
— Befuddled in Biloxi

A.   Dear *Befuddled*:
Well, if you ask various dressage riders, you will get different answers. Many believe that their horse "feels" the music and reacts to it. But others maintain that it is the rider that's reacting to the music and transferring that to the horse. Horses have acute hearing, through ears that rotate 180

degrees, so there is no doubt that they receive the music, but can they relate the beat of the music to the instructions that they are receiving from the rider? Here is an experiment that you can try. Next time that your wife is away, take her horse over to your neighbor's marijuana patch and let him graze there for awhile. Then let him loose in his paddock and blast some heavy metal music at it. Better still, play some of those old Dylan numbers. Then have a toke or two yourself. If you have vivid flash backs to the late 60s, early 70s, and can, like, really relate to the horse and the music, and the horse can, like, really, really relate to you, and you both eat every damn pellet of feed in the barn, then you have proved nothing except that the years have made you no smarter. You and the horse, however, will have developed a much closer relationship. What was the question again?

Snippets of Dressage History # LILX:
Origins of Prix St. Georges

As an internationally renowned expert on the history of dressage, I am often woken up at parties to clarify disputed points of the sport. Some of the more common questions posed to me are, "How did Prix St. Georges get its name?" and "How much alcohol is in that vodka martini?"

Well, the St. Georges in question is of course Saint George, the famous dragon slayer of legend. Our hero ranged around Medieval Europe slaying dragons and rescuing fair maidens in distress. The Saxon Chronicles, believed to be written by Saint Bede the Puerile, report, "The Lord's holy warrior saveth many a distraught maiden from a fate worseth than death itself, and, it is wrote, he saveth a couple for himself too." Saint George rode a magnificent gray Holsteiner, fully eighteen hands, named Asbestos, whose courage in the face of fire-breathing dragons was legendary. The Chronicles state, "When faceth a devil's monster, the great steed would lengthen the reins with goodly calmness by chewing of the bit whenever Saint George yieldeth the contact."

When there were no more dragons left to slay, Saint George and Asbestos turned their attention to wooly mammoths and saber-toothed tigers until they too were extinct. He then started in on the dodos and the passenger pigeons. Pretty soon Saint George became numero uno on the most wanted list of European conservationists, but he escaped to Russia, where he was such a big hit with the Tsarina, Catherine the horse lover, that she named Georgia after him.

Saint George and Asbestos loved to enter dressage competitions, but unfortunately Asbestos could never get the hang of piaffe and passage and the judges always marked them low. A special level, just below Intermediare I, that didn't require these difficult movements was developed and named for Saint George by his followers. Prix is an old Anglo-Saxon word that was added later to better illustrate the special relationship enjoyed between the judges and those self-same followers. Naturally, the pronunciation of the level was changed to Prix St. Georges in the French manner to ensure the elitist and ostentatious nature of the sport. So there you have it, Saint George, Holsteiner Asbestos, Wooly Mammoths and Prix: all part of the rich historical tapestry of the magnificent sport of dressage.
(Next installment — how to make a killer Vodka Martini).

Common Dressage Ailments
It only hurts when you ride

As I'm sure you are all too painfully aware, any activity that requires close proximity to horses carries with it a heightened risk of physical injury. Dressage riders are particularly vulnerable given the required sensitivity of the dressage horse, the amount of training essential to bring a dressage horse to competition standards, and the proclivity of dressage riders to do a lot of whining. For a sport that on the surface looks so pleasantly pastoral, so elegant and graceful, dressage is surprisingly dangerous. I suspect there are probably very few riders who enter a dressage ring without nursing one or more injuries, real or imaginary.

There are, of course, certain sports whose very nature requires that violence be committed upon the competition; such sports are boxing, football, ice hockey and, in the case of Tonya and Nancy, ladies' figure skating. And many sports, including dressage, have their own peculiar ailments. For example, in football and soccer there is the ubiquitous "groin injury." For some disturbing reason, my wife finds groin injuries among male athletes particularly amusing. When she enters the room and sees a football player or soccer player writhing in agony on the television screen, she always chuckles and asks, "Does that guy have a groin injury?" Other sports also have their own specific injuries that are actually named after the sport, such as tennis elbow, javelin throwers' impalement and weightlifters' toenail.

Veteran riders do not need to be reminded of the array of ailments specific to dressage, but I'm listing the major ones here anyway, presented as a warning to those young unwary souls who have recently been smitten with a passion for the sport.

Dressage Foot

This is caused by your horse stepping on your foot, which happens maybe twice a week, and is equivalent to someone smashing your foot with a large rock. The toes swell up like beach balls and eventually your feet will turn so many shades of purple, blue and red they will look like Walt Disney threw up on them. You will only be in pain when you walk.

Dressage Lower Back Syndrome

A universal equestrian ailment caused by the continuous crashing of the lower vertebrae into each other when trotting, which in turn causes the discs to squish out like peanut butter in a sandwich. This syndrome is exacerbated by tight boot syndrome before and after your ride, and if you also suffer from Dressage Foot, you will experience an exciting new world of pain. Away from the barn, your back will always ache, but the pain is acute when you cough or when you sit on the toilet. The only cure is surgery, where what's left of your discs can be scooped out and replaced with hockey pucks or pork chops.

Dressage Black Eye/Headache/Squint/Missing Teeth

Your horse suddenly turning his head and smacking it into your head causes these collective problems. I have personal experience of this, having once been sent flying across the stall by just the slightest flick of a horse's head. I came to several days later, and was told by my friends that I had spent the lost time approaching strangers, claiming that I was Vanna White and asking them if they wanted to buy a vowel. Of course the most serious injuries of this type occur when the horse kicks you, and I'm sorry to tell you that sooner or later, intentionally or otherwise, a horse is going to kick you. I must add that, alas, sooner or later you are going to fall off. It's best to fall off early in your dressage career, because when you reach the upper levels it's important for your prestige that you don't wear a hard hat in training. To the serious dressage rider, a slight skull fracture is preferable to being considered a dork by your peers.

Flat Chest Syndrome

This condition is prevalent among female riders who wear sports bras. Over time, these devilish devices cause the breasts to be pushed back into the chest and flattened. You should be aware that your overall appearance will be affected and your attractiveness to the opposite sex may be decreased, as a large portion of the male population believe that the female breast is the only tangible evidence of the existence of God. If you are a male rider who wears a sports bra, I'm afraid you have bigger problems to worry about than developing a flat chest.

Influenza, Pneumonia, Arthritis

These common afflictions are endemic in the equestrian world. Cold winter mornings mucking out stalls, stifling summer days clearing the paddocks or cleaning the tack are open invitations to any wandering virus. After you cool down your horse, who cools you down? Who puts a blanket on you when your bones chill, and who rigs up a fan to relieve your suffering? No one I know.

The English Twitch and the Scotch Hobble

They sound like exciting new dances, don't they? But these are very real and painful ailments. The English Twitch, often used by dressage veterans, is a self-inflicted injury caused by biting your lower lip in order to divert attention from more painful areas of your body. The Scotch Hobble is a chafing physical restraint placed on your legs by your fellow barn members immediately after a horse has kicked you, in order to prevent you skewering the animal with the closest pitchfork. The other type of Scotch Hobble, of course, is caused by drinking too much whiskey (if that's possible) and falling off the barstool.

Saddle Sores and Hemorrhoids

Yes, I'm afraid these afflictions are probably on your agenda. And you'll be stricken with a lot of them— which is why they are called piles.

Pre-Test Stress Syndrome

This is the terrible anxiety that builds up while you are in the warm-up area right before your test. It is a fear that your ride will be so bad that the photographer that you are paying to tape your test will keep the tape and send it to America's Funniest Home Videos. The symptoms of this distressing affliction include watery nasal discharge, weakness, stiffness, depression, difficulty in breathing and occasional flatulence. And that's just the horse. It is interesting to note that many of the more affluent dressage riders do not suffer from stress, but they are all carriers.

Horse Diseases transmitted to Humans

As if all of the above were not enough, there is an array of dangerous diseases that can be passed on to you by the very animals upon which you lavish so much love, time and money. These diseases are called zoonosis (honest!), and include Rabies, Salmonellosis, Anthrax, Tetanus, Tuberculosis and Brucellosis, or Bang's disease. "What is Bang's disease?" you ask quizzically. Apparently it's a disease that mainly affects cattle but horses are occasionally infected, where it is associated with fistula of the withers and poll evil. I have no clue what kind of illnesses fistula of the withers and poll evil are, but they sure as hell sound like something that I wouldn't want to catch. Imagine calling in sick to work and telling them that you've come down with a touch of fistula of the withers and poll evil. They'd give you a paid month off to make sure that you wouldn't infect the management team. Just poll evil on its own sounds like it could not only kill you but also send you straight to hell.

So, if you are a new dressage rider, these are all the afflictions that you can look forward to. And don't think your HMO is going cover them, because after you have finished paying your vet bills you won't be able to afford a bottle of aspirin let alone medical insurance.

One other thing. If you get the urge to find a boyfriend, you had better do it before you get too far along in your dressage career. Otherwise, what he will see is an arthritic female hobbling along with missing teeth, nasal discharge, a flat chest, a black eye, a swollen lip, possibly suffering from poll evil, and smelling like a horse. Other than that, you will probably appear quite attractive.

Are Horses Smarter than Men?
A rhetorical question examined

I know what you are thinking, "What a stupid question. Of course horses are smarter than men—why is it even up for discussion? A piece of stale pound cake is smarter than most men." Well, not so fast, little Miss Clever-Knickers, there are two sides to every issue. So let's put aside our biases, shall we; let's stow our baggage in the attic for a moment; let's file our personnel experiences in the suspended folder; and let's look at this issue through the cold filter of absolute objectivity. Nah, that's no fun—go up to the attic and bring that baggage back down.

Consider this: I'm mucking out the stalls, and a horse is in his standing paddock with his head stuck over the open Dutch door staring at me. His stare means "Hey, when are you going to be finished because I want to get at that hay in the corner and I really need to urinate." And I'm thinking, God forbid the beast should have to relieve himself in his pasture. I'm getting pressure from a horse, for crying out loud, so you tell me which one of us is smarter? Who controls whom? Who works for whom? I have to feed myself, clean up my own mess, wash myself, make my own bed, braid my own hair (not that my hair is braided you understand, but if it was, no animal that I know is going to do it for me).

Consider this also: I'm over in England visiting a famous racetrack in the town of Newmarket, which you may have heard of, particularly if you are a Dick Francis fan. For some strange reason, the racetrack and training facilities are on one side of the town, but the stables are on the other side of the town. Every day when the horses go out for training they have to be ridden through the center of a very busy town, which requires them to negotiate several traffic signals. The button for pedestrians to push to change the lights is not at the normal level, however, it's at the level of a jockey on a horse (honest), and can't be

reached unless you are as tall as a basketball player. So I'm standing at this set of traffic lights for ten minutes waiting for a horse to come along so that I can cross the road. Now you tell me—who is the dummy?

Not that you need further proof, but compare the behaviors of men that you know to those of your horse, and see who comes out with an IQ lower than gorgonzola, and smelling worse. It's no contest. For example: horses don't drink beer until they fall over, horses don't voluntarily get tattoed, they don't remember all the words to *Baby, I Need Your Lovin'*, and, of course, they don't bet on horse races. You'll never look in your rear view mirror and notice that a horse is driving the car that has been tailgating you for the last six miles. A jackass maybe, but not a horse. Most male horses don't spend 95% of their lives thinking about sex—you've probably made sure of that. There are certain behaviors, however, that men and horses share. For example, they both eat gross food, they both bite and occasionally slobber, they both think the world is their urinal and, compared to women, they both haven't got a clue.

Just to give this whole discussion a slight semblance of objectivity, let us outline the case against the intelligence of horses. I've heard it said that horses are so stupid that they will keep eating feed until they colic and die. I guess that is pretty stupid if it's true, but it's not that much worse than human behavior at an all-you-can-eat buffet, particularly here in the land of fatty tissue. But the biggest and much-stated argument for the stupidity of horses is that if they were smart, they wouldn't allow people to ride on their backs. They wouldn't have taken the abuse that men have dished out to them over the centuries (and when I say men I don't mean humans—I mean the male of the species specifically). It's another measure of the depths of evil to which men can plunge when you consider how dreadfully these beautiful creatures have been treated for millennia. Always wanting to please their masters, they have been used and misused as beasts of burden, as transportation, as food, as sport, as cavalry. I wonder how many millions of innocent horses have died in battle, helping to satisfy man's bloodlust? As an example, Napoleon's invasion of Russia in 1812 was such a total disaster not because of the army that he lost—he assembled another large army the following year. It was because he left half a million of his horses dead in the Russian snow, and they were irreplaceable.

Today, thankfully, most horses are treated decently and dressage horses, as you are well aware, are lovingly pampered. So, here is a theory for your consideration. Suppose, back in prehistory, the ancestors of horses realized at some point that they were facing extinction. Maybe some new powerful predator had evolved and horses, being large animals with thin fragile legs, were easy prey. In fact, that predator could well have been humans. Now, about this time, humankind were making the transition from hunter/gatherers to farmers, and horses saw an opportunity to avoid extinction. I'm not suggesting that they formed committees or focus groups to study the problem, although I can picture that, can you? But instinctively, through some type of genetic communication fired by the overwhelming urge for their species to survive, they collectively allowed themselves to become domesticated. Perhaps that was their only option to prevent extinction—after all, horse ancestors had already become extinct in the Americas. Maybe they sensed that if they became indispensable to humans, and horses were, until recently, the most indispensable of all domesticated animals—then they would be fed, housed and protected by this new aggressive species of animal. Sure, they would also be abused occasionally and, sure, they would have to work hard, but being domesticated by man allowed them to effectively step out of the food chain. That's pretty damn smart.

It's also not beyond the bounds of possibility that horses sensed that they would only have to be men's servants for a just a couple of clicks of the evolutionary clock. Maybe intuitively they know that humans only showed up last Tuesday in geological time and, as a result of their self-destructive behavior, will be gone by next Thursday. A week from Sunday there will not a trace left to show that humans were here—an evolutionary biochemical experiment gone terribly wrong. But horses will still be around—larger, stronger and smarter thanks to humans selectively breeding them. Hey, after all the humans have gone, maybe the horses will throw a big party. They might call it, "The Plan Worked" party, and invite all the sheep, cows, pigs, goats and chickens. Pretty far-fetched, I know, but on the next occasion when you and your horse have some quiet time together, take a long hard look into the back of his eyes. You might experience a momentary, yet terrifying, awareness of being used. It may very well be that horses are even smarter than women.

Snippets of Dressage History # XIVCDI:
Paul Revere's big night out

Listen my children and you shall hear
Of the midnight ride of Paul Revere,
He said to his friend, "If the British embark
One if by land, and two if by sea,
And three if by Delta Airlines from Newark
And I on the opposing lead will be."

Tales of the Wayside Inn — Longfellow (kinda')

Have you ever wondered about the origins and the meanings of the letters that mark out a dressage ring? Why, of course you have, my little cauliflowers. While there are as many countries as flies in a feed bucket that claim the origin—Germany, Holland, Denmark and Mozambique among them—the actual origin comes from the good old U.S. of A.—right here in New England, as a matter of fact. Here, then, is the truth, straight from the warmblood's mouth.

As you undoubtedly remember from your high school history class, Paul Revere was a courageous American patriot, a talented silversmith and a legendary drunk, but you may not be aware that he was also an excellent dressage rider. He is not celebrated for his dressage skills, however, but for the fact that he was responsible for warning the local Massachusetts minutemen that the British were coming (as if those bright red uniforms were not a dead giveaway). Paul's famous ride took place during the preliminary rounds of the American Revolution, which involved a monumental struggle blah, blah, blah, blah, blah.

Anyway, on a dark night before Micklemas, it was discovered that British troops were on their way to Boston to sort out the local troublemakers. Fortunately, the British were held up by customs officials at Boston Harbor while they were being disinfected for Foot and Mouth, (the British—not the customs officials) which bought some time for the local patriots to prepare. Meanwhile, Paul and his buddies were getting tanked up in Sam Adams' local tavern until their leaders, Colonel Ethan Allen and Colonel Jordan Marsh, rounded up the men, ordered them to mount up and lined them in a row in front of the Old North Church.

The Colonels needed a courageous volunteer to ride out to the suburbs to warn all the Investment Analysts, Personal Trainers and Soccer Moms that live there. They asked for one rider to take four steps forward. Unfortunately, Paul Revere's faithful horse, Prudential, had never mastered the four steps back routine. So when every other rider reined in four steps, Paul and Prudential were left alone up front, proud though unwitting volunteers. Paul, still drunk as a skunk, set off on his historic ride. The year was seventeen hundred and something or other.

Paul's first stop was at Fenway Park, where the New York Yankees were in the process of knocking the Red Sox out of playoff contention. Next, Paul headed to Boston Gardens, where the Celtics had just been thrashed by the Philadelphia Twenty-Sixes, and all the fans were standing around waiting for Bill Russell and Larry Bird to be born. Paul Revere decided not to head down to Foxboro where the Patriots were being embarrassed by the East Virginia Ruffians. It was all too depressing.

So Paul started down the central divider on the Massachusetts Turnpike, starting in **A**rlington and stopping in E**X**eter, where he saluted to the local populace. (I know, I know—the Mass Turnpike doesn't go to Arlington or Exeter. Well, in those days it did.) Paul decided to make a note of all the towns through which he rode, and to practice his dressage tests on the way. So he did a 30m circle in **S**udbury, an extended trot across the diagonal to **F**ramingham, a collected walk from there to **M**illis and a strong yet lucid passage to **H**opkinton. His shoulder-in from there to **K**ingston was fluent and cohesive, though it lacked impulsion as they passed **B**rockton. Hey, it's a long way from Hopkinton to Brockton to be doing a shoulder-in! Rider and horse performed a perfect canter pirouette at **D**racut, etc,etc. (I hope that you've gotten the gist of this by now, because frankly I'm getting tired of pushing my little arrow up to the **Bold** key). Paul and Prudential finally ended their historic ride in **C**oncord at the home of the famous revolutionary chicken (*see below for a fascinating explanation).

Thanks to Paul, the Minutemen were ready in—well, in a minute, and those pesky British hooligans got their

comeuppance. He handed the piece of paper with his notes on to Colonel Ethan Allen who stuck it on the wall of the Cheers Pub on Boston Common. A couple of months later, the pub was captured by Hessians during the battle of Filenes Basement, who later took Paul's paper back to Hesse in Germany. There it was used to lay out the first official dressage ring, letters and all, allowing the Germans to get a leg up on the rest of the world, dressage-wise. Paul's dressage test itself was thought by many to be the most important in history, although it was marked very low, probably because Paul dismounted at every transition to wet his whistle at the local alehouse. So now you know the rest of the story. That is where the letters came from—accept no other explanations.

* *Few people are aware of the statue to honor the revolutionary chicken in Concord, located off the beaten path, just to the left of the Old North Bridge. The story goes that, in the early days of the American Revolution, a group of Tories who were loyal to the Crown heard that the*

Minutemen had a secret musket cache hidden in Concord. They planned to steal these arms and sneaked into the town in the dead of night. As they quietly passed a chicken coop, however, they inadvertently awoke the rooster who began squawking will all his might. This racket awoke the Minutemen who ran out and seized all of the Tories. The arms were saved and a statue was erected to honor the brave chicken that had raised the alarm. The inscription on the bottom of the statue reads: "Here Lies the Original Chicken Cacciatore!"

Creative Manure Management
Yankee ingenuity at its best

Here is another article about horse manure. My wife says that I write far too much stuff about manure to be considered psychologically healthy. That may be so, but I have to shovel the damn stuff every day, she just has to step over it, so I'm bound to have more of an affinity to it. Maybe though, just maybe, she is right and I've developed some kind of bizarre obsession for it. Don't you love it when you discover that you're even weirder than you think you are?

Growing up on the Liverpool Docklands, the only horse that we kids ever saw was the poor old nag that pulled the cart of the Rag and Bone man. This was the tinker that came around every week to buy anything, just anything, from people who had nothing. Sometimes we kids would find or 'borrow' something that had a slight value, such as a house brick, and the Rag and Bone man would give us a goldfish for it. We always ate the goldfish that night.

No, just kidding, we would put the goldfish in an empty jam jar, fill it with tap water, drop in a couple of Cornflakes for food, and the next morning the goldfish would be dead. Then we would eat it. But if the Rag and Bone man had nothing to buy and we had nothing to sell, the Rag and Bone man's horse had something for free that everyone seemed to want—manure. As soon as the deed was done, all the local housewives would rush out of their tenements and scoop the stuff up, to spread on their paltry little vegetable patches, or many even to just spread on their poultry. Anyway, the stuff clearly had some intrinsic value, in that time and in that place.

Now over four decades later, here on our little horse property (the property is little, not the horses) located in the Massachusetts boonies, we have enough of the stuff to boggle the imagination. We only have two horses but they both produce twice their own weight in manure every day—a fact that would absolutely astound me if I hadn't just made it up. Nevertheless, our manure pile is large enough to interfere with cell phone transmissions. And we can't get rid of the stuff. Living in a town with 5000 people and 400 horses, the local market for horse manure is glutted to say the least. There are only a limited number of garden stores, farm stands and rose growers around, and our property is not big enough to have anywhere to spread it.

So every Labor Day weekend, my wife and I hire a Bobcat and a 30-foot dumpster and spend quality time heaving the stuff from the manure pile into the bin. My wife actually looks forward to this endeavor, because she has so much fun working the Bobcat. "Whee," she goes "Wheeee—I want one of these for Christmas," as she bangs wheelies in the mud. I, on the other hand, am simply not amused, because I have to stand inside the dumpster raking the stuff smooth as she dumps it in (please don't tell anyone that I used to work with). By the end of the weekend, we are out close to $1000 for rental fees, my body aches like it's been caught in a rhino stampede, and my wife is thoroughly exhilarated. There must be a better way, I think. There must be an easier and less expensive way of disposing of horse manure. So I asked my acquaintances in the dressage world what creative ways they could think of to use it. None of them had a worthwhile opinion and they all moved away from me slowly, which means little, as they tend to move away from me slowly whatever the circumstances. Undeterred, here are some brilliant ideas of my own, designed to cash in on unwanted horse poop.

1. **Christmas Ornaments**. I know, this is kind of obvious, so I thought that I'd get it out of the way first. Basically, you just put the droppings in your kitchen freezer for a couple of days, then spray each one with shellac, sprinkle with glittery stuff, tie a little ribbon around it and hang it from your Christmas tree. What a festive and practical way to fill in those cold December nights! Invite your friends over to toast your ingenuity with some spiced eggnog, and maybe have a little intervention session. I guarantee you that a lot of dressage people would purchase these, particularly if they came from a famous horse. (Someone once told me that some cool dude had come up with the idea of carving dried horse manure into little chickadees and calling them bird turds! Now, that's the type of person you'd want in your lifeboat).

2. **Riot Control**. Whenever the corporate criminals have gotten together recently to carve up the pie a little bit

finer amongst themselves, outraged demonstrators have gathered en masse to let them know that there are still people with conscience that care about something other than the almighty dollar. Of course, their demonstrations will have no effect other than to make good coverage for the six o'clock news and to allow the police to shoot off their water cannon and rubber bullets. So why not arm the demonstrators with some really fresh horse dung? It's just the right size for throwing (not that I've tried that, you understand).

3. **Vandalism**. While we are on the subject of lobbing the stuff at people, here is an idea. Take all the kids that vandalize or continually commit minor felonies, stand them up against a wall and have their victims chuck horse manure at them for five minutes. That'll bring them down a peg or two, and might even prove to be a deterrent. I'll be happy to beta test this idea on the kids that keep smashing my mailbox.

4. **Land Reclamation**. You've got to hand it to the Dutch: not only are they great dressage riders but they also have literally carved their country out of the sea. The very word *Netherland* means *underwater* in German. I'm sure that they would be very thankful if we filled up a couple of dozen Exxon oil tankers with horse poop and shipped it over to them. They could dump the stuff in the North Sea and almost double the size of their country in no time. They might even reach as far as England, although the Dutch might not find any particular advantage in that. Still, think of the size of the tulips they could grow. Plus, whenever one of those pesky holes appears in the dykes, there would be no need to search around for some poor Dutch lad, just bung in a horse turd. A dung bung!

5. **Landscaping**. I don't mean local garden stuff or golf courses (although the thought of covering the nation's golf courses with horse manure is very gratifying). I'm talking about the Midwest—all those states that end in vowels and are as flat as a dressage husband's wallet. I imagine they would be so grateful for a few hills that the smell wouldn't bother them at all. Just spray the hills with hydro seeding and before you can say "Religious Right-Wing Creationists," the landscape would be as varied and lush as the Welsh hills. And without all that annoying singing. Mind you, they would have to be careful not to build anything on them.

6. **Doggie Treats**. I know that I said earlier that these were all my ideas—well, I lied. This particular suggestion came from a dressage acquaintance , and it is so obvious that I'm mad that I didn't think of it myself. Anyone who spends anytime around a barn, and there are almost always dogs around, know how irresistible the stuff is to them. My dog, Gromit, considers our manure heap his own personal twenty-four buffet. I know that you non-horse types are currently sticking your fingers down your throats and going "Ugh, ugh, gross, disgusting." Well, it isn't so disgusting when you figure that in parts of the Southwest, people actually have contests to see how far they can throw cow patties. Which explains a lot, I suppose. I think that they have even applied for it to become an Olympic Event in 2008, and apparently they have a good chance of getting it included. (You just have to flash a few American dollars at those Olympic Honchos and you could get "Synchronized Underwater Dental Flossing" included). Anyway, according to my vet, the stuff doesn't do dogs any

harm. So this one gets my vote, and I'll soon be in the doggie treat business. Keep your eyes peeled in your local pet store and soon you will find "Hearty Hanoverian Hunks," "Delicious Warmblood Woofers," and "Danish Doo-Doo Drops."

So there you have it, I've managed to write another article about horse manure, and I couldn't be prouder. If you have any good ideas that you think should be included, please send them along to me. Don't be discouraged and dump your ideas if someone poo-poos them. You need to get them out of your system, so if your suggestions need flushing out, together we can get to the bottom of the problem. This article has now definitely gone in the toilet. Sorry.

Advanced Clicker Clinic for Dressage Husbands
Improving your relationship without words

Brian McKeown
Clinic correspondent

The much-anticipated inaugural "Advanced Clicker Clinic for Dressage Husbands" took place last week at Milksop Farm in Koldass, Illinois, and by all accounts was a huge success. With its origins in southern California, clicker training for dressage spouses has swept across the country of late, and is now being exported into the major European dressage countries. Many well-regarded American dressage officials believe that transitioning clicker training commands from horses to husbands is probably the most important contribution that the United States has made to the sport of dressage, so far.

It was no surprise, then, that the first advanced clicker clinic was overwhelmed with applicants. Clinic organizer, Teresa Throttle, reported that 40 couples were accepted for the three-day clinic, with an additional 350 couples paying top dollar to act as auditors. The training was performed by two famous clinicians, ex-Navy Seal Nancy Knuckler and Dr. Elsie Borgia, both graduates of the Lorena Bobbit College of Husband Husbandry in Chicago, Illinois.

A prerequisite for acceptance in the clinic was that all participants must have completed the basic course of clicker training. So, by way of a refresher, the first hour was spent emphasizing the seven basic commands of clicker training for dressage husbands: *Sit, Fetch, Work Hard, Shower, Don't Touch, Shut up* and *Sign This Check*. Then Ms. Knuckler demonstrated how to use the little yellow clicker in a sort of Morse Code format to communicate more complex commands such as *Run my bath, Clean out the trailer* and *Wash the windows*. She spoke of how clicker training can revolutionize communication between dressage riders and their partners. "Verbal communication is so often tragically misunderstood," Ms. Knuckler stated. "You have to be extremely careful which words are emphasized, and the very tone of your voice, if not precisely tempered, can elicit the wrong response. And we all know that most men are a little dim, anyway," she chuckled. "With the clicker, however, such complex demands as, *'I'll have another gin and tonic while you're up,'* or even the more difficult, *'Go and get another home equity loan,'* can soon be easily understood, without the use of actual words." She concluded, "there is no more moving sight to behold than when a woman presses that little clicker a couple of times and her slathering husband leaps into action, eager to please."

Clinic participant Charles Tadcaster agrees. A

forty-year-old computer programmer gelding from Philadelphia, Charles credits clicker training for saving his marriage. "My wife is from the South," he explained, "plus she drinks a bit, so sometimes her words become so slurred that I'm not sure exactly what she wants me to do. The problem reached a crisis point one evening last summer when she ordered me to get her an *Ast Tee*. She was actually asking for an iced tea, but I thought she wanted some Asti Spumanti so I rushed out to the liquor store. She was furious, and rightly so. It was then that I knew clicker training was the only answer, and since then our relationship is back on track."

On the second day, Dr. Borgia concentrated on teaching multiple commands, which required more diligence and focus from both clickor and clickee. Intricate double commands included *Stop dithering and drag the arena*, *Take this movie back and rent one that I might like* and *We are lost—stop and ask for directions*. This last one appeared very difficult for most of the husbands to grasp.

A small brouhaha developed in mid-morning when one husband, Jeremy Jaffa from Tampa Bay, broke loose and began running around the parking lot. "LOOSE HUSBAND, LOOSE HUSBAND!" the cry went up, as clinic officials, armed with halters, chased the man down. He was soon subdued and brought back into his wife's custody. Clearly shaken, Jeremy explained, "When my wife first told me that we were going to take clicker training, I naturally assumed that I was going to learn how to operate the dozen or so remote controls that we have laying around the house. I never expected this—please let me go home."

At the end of the day, all participants took part in

a joint review of what they had learned so far. Most husbands easily interpreted the commands *Clean my boots, Brush my shadbelly* and *Scrub the water buckets*, although one poor fellow got all three commands mixed up, then tried to scrub his wife's belly with Kiwi shoe polish. Another unfortunate hubby misinterpreted the command *Spray the horse* for *Spay the horse*, and ran around in a circle totally confused, hardly surprising given that he was an investment analyst and the horse was a gelding.

The final day concentrated on overcoming spousal resistance, or pushback, to clicker commands. Ms. Knuckler emphasized that any resistance must be overcome immediately when it is encountered. She encouraged dressage wives to always be vigilant to the signs of resistance, such as muttering under the breath or lethargic responsiveness. She warned that signs of agitation when he is vacuuming the carpets, for example, could quickly deteriorate into the syndrome known as "Hoover rage." Withholding of privileges generally will curb minor resistance, Dr. Borgia advised, while more serious problems can be dealt with by resorting to the whip. She cautioned, however, that the whip must be used prudently, as overuse can sometimes result in the husband becoming used to it, and in some instances, even enjoying it. In which case, it can then be used as a reward.

Another problem to avoid, Dr. Borgia instructed, was the mixing of clickers. While dog clickers, horse clickers and husband clickers all look the same, they have slightly different tones. They cannot be interchanged and it is essential, she urged, that they not be inadvertently mixed. A lady in Tennessee reported that, while trying to impress her friends, she mistakenly used her dog clicker on her husband, resulting in him running out into the yard and urinating on her rhododendrons. More tragically, another incident occurred when Valerie Sawtoothe and her husband were visiting the Grand Canyon. Valerie intended to signal her husband to remove the lens cap from their camera but she erroneously used her horse clicker and gave the command to rein back. Her husband took four steps backward and disappeared over the Canyon wall. The incident ended happily, however, when Valerie purchased a Grand Prix Dutch Warmblood with the insurance money.

Finally, the instructors emphasized the importance of providing rewards for positive behavior. They suggested that rewards such as a light beer now and then, or even allowing a husband to watch the Cooking Channel, not forgetting the occasional peppermint, were ample. Some of the husbands stated that, quite frankly, that was not the type of reward they were hoping for.

Everyone present (except poor Jeremy) agreed that the clinic was time extremely well spent and would hopefully be the first of many. Prizes were presented to the participants who had progressed the most, including the coveted "golden clicker" awarded to Margaret Mangle who, using her new found clicker skills, had taken just twenty minutes to teach her husband how to braid. The female participants practiced their new found skills as they left, clicking furiously to see whose husband would be first to bring their SUV around to the arena entrance.

Further advanced clicker clinics are planned for Des Moines, Wichita, Chattanooga and... wait a second, there is a noise coming from the living room. I have to go, now. Bye.

A Faux Pas at NEDA Fall
Helping the judges with their comments

This article first appeared in the November 2000 edition of the New England Dressage Association's newsletter **A Tip of the Hat.** *It caused quite a furor because a few folks took it seriously.*

The board of the New England Dressage Association has asked me to apologize to its members for what it has termed my "inappropriate behavior" at the recent NEDA Fall Show.

I sincerely regret any offense that may have been endured by the competitors based on any inappropriate comments on my part. I am particularly concerned that the judges would be offended by any misunderstanding that my comments in any way reflected their views of the riders and horses that they were there to assess.

I attended the NEDA Fall show as a volunteer assuming naturally that my status as a world renown expert on dressage history would qualify me for a special booth, where I would answer complex historical dressage queries posed by admiring dressage groupies. To my indignation, I was instead assigned the job as Scorer. This required me to sit in a hut and add up the riders' scores from each dressage test, by punching in the numbers into an adding machine and then passing them to the person sitting next to me for verification. The person sitting next to me, who happened to be my wife, would correct my mistakes (a skill that she has perfected over the years) and then pass the test to the person who would publish the results of each class. You can imagine the overwhelming boredom that I was subjected to by being involved in such a task, not to mention the criminal waste of my knowledge and talent. Naturally, my mind searched for something— anything—to overcome the ennui. I decided that I would embellish the judges' comments summarized at the end of each test. A decision, I now realize, lacked a degree of prudence.

So, I must apologize to the rider, placed last in the Training Level, Test 1, to whose judge's comments I added, "The lucidity of your impulsion is unfortunately offset by the irregularity of your transitions." Further, the comment that I added to the test of the winner of the Grand Prix, "Get a life," was also totally inappropriate. The indignant reaction of the two young ladies who performed the entertaining Pas de Deux is also understandable, where I stated, "Your your coordination coordination is is commendable commendable but but your your cadenced cadenced strides strides require require further further suppleness suppleness."

If any of the following comments appeared on your test then, more than likely, they were mine and not those of your judges. You then fall under the umbrella of this apology.

"My advice to you is: try taking up quilting."

"Your canter pirouette demonstrated the head coming through without engagement behind, swinging hindquarters, labored strides, plus the sequence and rhythm of the canter was lost. Otherwise it was great."

"You displayed all the grace and suppleness of a fried clam."

"On the bit, above the bit, on the bit, above the bit—make up your mind."

"More pizzazz in your passage, and more pep in your piaffe."

"Your flying change should be light, bold and cadenced so that the period of suspension is pronounced. For this reason, slightly less collection is called for than in your normal collected canter." (Just to show you that I can cook when I want!).

"For Prix St. Georges, you rode a great Second Level test."

"Your transitions were almost Presbyterian in their pretensions."

"Save your smiles for the male judges—that stuff doesn't work on me."

Once again, I deeply regret these and other improper comments, made even worse by the fact that I was sober when I made them. I blame no one but myself, and perhaps the devil, and am ashamed to have detracted from the solemn ostentation of the sport of dressage.

Snippets of Dressage History # XCIVLI:
The origins of piaffe

To the dressage aficionado, there is no spectacle more beautiful to behold than a top level rider, atop a top level horse, performing the classic piaffe movement. Extremely difficult to master, piaffe involves the horse executing an exaggerated trot without moving forward, which requires that the horse responds to contradictory commands—move forward at the trot, at the same time not moving forward. This accounts for the popular belief that many top-level riders do not know whether they are coming or going.

Many dressage experts mistakenly believe that the term *piaffe* is derived from the French word *piaffer* that translated means to step. To these so-called experts I say *bouche mon derrière* that translated means, "I beg to differ." The dressage movement piaffe is actually named after the famous French singer Edith Piaf, affectionately known by her multitude of fans as the little rodent—or maybe it was the little sparrow.

Edith Piaf was born somewhere in France on 19 December 1915. Originally named Edith Passage, her father was a circus acrobat who taught her the art of vaulting before she could walk. However, because of her youth, she kept falling off the horse and was in danger of being trampled on the next pass because...well, because she couldn't walk. To help her along, her father abandoned her in a cheap Normandy brothel where she spent her formative years learning many of life's important lessons, such as how to get pregnant at age sixteen.

Soon Edith was out on the street, singing for her supper, begging from strangers. Because she had a voice that could curdle butter, Edith was quickly discovered by Louis Leplee, a Parisian impresario, who booked her into the famous Alhambra nightclub in January 1937. Her first successful recording was "Mon Legionnaire" (*translation—My Disease*), which hit the number one slot in Finland, followed by "C'est lui que mon Coeur a choisi" (*Oh, Yes, We have no Bananas*). Edith was now on her way. She became the number one nightclub singer in Paris, in the Adult Amateur, Fourth Level, French Warmblood class. In the winter of 1940, she fell in love with a young singer named Paul Meurisse. He was the only man in her life, except for Jean Cocteau, Jean-Louis Barrault, Serge Reggiani and Norbert Glanzberg. Also there were Lou Barrier, Yves Montand, Marcel Cerdan, Eddie Constantine, Charles Aznavour and Jaques Pills. Not forgetting Felix Martin, Douglas Davis, Georges Moustaki, Theo Sarapo and the 1951 French Cycling Team, to name but a few.

During World War II, Edith toured the Stalags, singing to prisoners and helping many to escape. She would disguise them as Maurice Chevalier and smuggle them out, claiming they were a double act. When the Germans finally caught her, they punished her by forcing her to gargle with kitty litter (unused—thankfully). Unwittingly, her captors had perfected the unique gravelly texture of her voice, for which she will never be forgotten, no matter how hard you might try. After the war, Edith toured America where critics likened her to Judy Garland with a really bad sinus infection. Returning to Paris, she recorded many of her most unforgettable classics, such as "*Neuf Garcons, un Coeur*" (Nine Waiters—One Table) and "*Non, Je ne Regrette Rien*" (I Could Care Less).

Edith loved dressage, but being only knee high to a grasshopper, she was able to ride only very small horses. It was on her famous Shetland Pony, Fromage, that she perfected the famous movement that now bears her name. Why, you ask, are 'Piaf' and 'piaffe' spelled differently? Where did the extra 'fe' come from? Look, I can't be expected to know everything now, can I? So there you have it, ma cheri: Edith, Yves Montand, Fromage, kitty litter, cycling teams— all part of the rich tapestry of the wonderful sport of Dressage.

(Send $29.95 plus tax for a copy of this Snippet with all the French accents added).

Home is where the Horse Is
Whole lotta shakin' in Harvard Yard

It is not Sin City, that's for sure. It lacks the exotic, erotic appeal of, say, a Bangkok or the steaming, teeming excitement of Rio by night. There are no famous opera houses, no castles or chateaux dripping with history, no ancient ruins (unless you count the tool shed at the end of our yard). Its very name does not conjure up mystery or intrigue, romance or adventure. We are not talking Hong Kong, Casablanca or Katmandu. We are talking Harvard, Massachusetts, hometown to my missus, her two Swedish Warmbloods, and yours truly.

The town of Harvard thrives about 30 miles due west of Boston, and has little or no association with the university of the same name, except they were both founded by the same two dudes, Nathan Harvard the swineherd and his cousin, John Hancock the insurance salesman. Although a major highway, Route 495, cuts a black swath through the middle of the town, Harvard remains a bucolic, apple-infested, idyllic example of what a typical New

England township ought to be. It's a small, upper middle class community populated by prestigious Liberal Democrats (except for seven shamefaced Republicans and one rabid Socialist just a little left of Trotsky, who might be me) with wholesome families and wholesome family pets. A damn fine place to live, if the truth be known.

If you have been working your butt to a frazzle all year and are looking for a quiet, restful vacation where you can just simply sleep for a week, then you can't do better than to come stay in Harvard. That is, if we had a hotel, which we don't. Neither do we have a grocery store, a video store, a Starbucks—no industry of any sort, just lots of old stone walls and beautiful pine trees. There is no low cost housing in Harvard, nor do we want any, although we believe passionately that such housing should be made available in other towns. On second thought, maybe you shouldn't come here because, frankly, we really don't want riff-raff the likes of you coveting our quaint New England heritage houses or tromping through our conservation areas. That is unless you own a horse. If you own a horse or just simply love horses, then you will be welcomed with open arms, because Harvard is horse country.

In a small town of 5,000 souls, we have 400 horses. You can smell Harvard from Delaware (on the other hand, you can smell Delaware from California). Almost everyone who lives here owns a horse; many of them housed in their backyards or their guest bedrooms. Harvard attracts horse lovers like the Fortune 500 management attracts crooks. And there are many horse farms here. Priscilla Endicott resides here, still operating her famous dressage school, "The Ark." An American dressage doyenne and a really nice person, Priscilla is renowned for her wonderful book **Taking up the Reins: A Year in Germany**. She is currently working on a sequel, **Letting Down your Guard: A Weekend in Reno**. Kathy Connelly also calls Harvard home, at her horse farm, Apple Valley. Kathy, a one-time U.S. representative in the dressage World Cup and a renowned trainer, is one of my favorite dressage friends. She once told me that the secret to a successful relationship with a dressage queen is to take the blame for everything. Advice that I credit in no small way with helping the longevity of my marriage. At one time or another, Sue Blinks trained in Harvard, and Walter Christenson taught here. So Harvard is to horses what navels are to lint.

It is an offense in Harvard for an automobile to spook a horse on the roadway, or to even drive too close or too fast. I'll bet you like *that* law. Forty-five percent of the town is conservation land, so we have more horse trails than the state of Montana, without any weird macho survivalists. But there is more to Harvard than horses. It was here, several grandmothers ago in the late eighteenth century, that a healthy Shaker community established itself.

Now if any religious sect had a good news/bad news message to impart it was the Shakers. The good news was that their ceremonies involved a lot of dancing. It seems to me that any religion that required you to shake your booty must have had a lot to offer, particularly to those of us who believe that any Supreme Being (or Beings) cannot possibly take themselves seriously. The Shakers' bad news of course was that all of their members were required to be celibate. Not just the leaders—everyone. The Shakers' founder, Mother Ann Lee (no surprise that the founder of a no-sex religion was a woman) decreed that saying nix to hanky-panky would make your entry through the pearly gates go a whole lot smoother. Then she sat down with her followers and wondered why her religion was dying out. Well, Duh! By 1918, all of the Harvard Shakers had gone to the big hoe-down in the sky, leaving behind for posterity, a lot of really boring furniture.

To its credit, the town of Harvard has preserved its historic Shaker heritage including the original Shaker village and the Holy Hill of Zion, atop which the Shakers used to perform their religious ceremonies. A beautiful wooded trail winds up Holy Hill to a flat quarter acre at the summit known as the Holy Place, bounded by a small white fence and sparkling birch trees. If you stand near the spot where the Holy Stone was once placed, you can envision the scene on an eighteenth century autumn Sunday morning with the sun streaming through the trees on the Shakers below, boppin' and a-hoppin' in the crisp New England air. The guys would line up on one side and the gals on the other side separated by about ten yards. I'll bet they had a big sign nailed to one of the trees that said, "Look but don't Touch." The music that they danced to was quite upbeat, not those heavy, mournful dirges usually associated with most religions. It wasn't exactly Jerry Lee Lewis (although *Whole Lotta Shakin' Goin' On* would have been appropriate); it was closer to, say, Procul Harum.

If your horse can handle the hill, it is a magical trail ride up the narrow path to the Holy Place, then descending on the other side to circle around at the base for a long and wonderful woodland amble back to the parking lot, forty five minutes later. Nary a living soul will you meet, but the spirits of the Shakers are all around and will guide your horse's hooves. Ride alone and you will experience a higher awareness level—a wonderful feeling of peace and contentment. You need not be concerned with disturbing the Shakers' spirits—they must have been sufficiently disturbed to have joined the religion in the first place.

My dog Gromit and I trek up Holy Hill once or twice a week, and I think Gromit can actually see the Shaker spirits, like that kid in the movie *The Sixth Sense*, particularly when we reach the Holy Place. It seems such a wonderfully serene place that I often think it's a great pity that the Shaker religion has died out. Occasionally, Gromit and I will dance around the spot where the Holy Stone once rested (the Stone is gone now, a victim of poxy vandals) in the hope that the spirits may show themselves. Their failure to do so I have to lay at Gromit's doorstep because, frankly, his dancing ability is embarrassingly stiff, even for a Golden Retriever. Sometimes I think: why does a street urchin from the Liverpool Docklands find himself fifty years later living in Harvard, Massachusetts, pulled by some irresistible force to the Shaker's Holy Hill? Is it coincidence or is it just Kismet, pure and simple?

Could it be that the Shaker spirits long for a resurgence of their religion? Are they searching for a new leader, another Mother Ann Lee, a modern charismatic Chosen One to build their religion anew and carry it proudly, yet reverently, into this new millennium? Well, Mother Ann, I'm your man (figuratively speaking, of course). If it's a resurgence you want, it's a resurgence I'm here to deliver. I'm afraid that the furniture will have to go, but the dancing, of course, will stay. That's a major recruiting point. You'll be surprised to learn that I would keep the no sex rule, but with a slight modification. Total celibacy in this life, but all the nooky you want in the next. That's why it's called heaven. What do you say, friends—shall I sign you up?

Fancy French Phrasology
How to parlez-vous avec les crème de la crème

It has come to my attention that certain of our brother dressage spouses are experiencing difficulties in assimilating into the more sophisticated world of dressage elitists as their wives move up the levels, and consequently up the social ladder. Whether you are a beer-swilling, blue-collar couch potato or a stodgy, one-dimensional financial consultant, it is important that you don't become an embarrassment to your loving wife, or to us, your fellow suffering brethren.

If you wish for your wife's riding friends to admire and respect you, then you must ensure your conversational skills project you as a cultured, cosmopolitan man-about-town. This will demonstrate that you are indeed *one of them*. I don't mean literally one of them (not that there is anything wrong with that, you understand). I mean that you can hold your own in any group of cultivated equestrians. I don't mean literally *hold your own*, that would constitute a major embarrassment to everyone around you, unless you are a baseball player. So, once again, here I am, Mr. Dressage Husband to the rescue, with sound advice on how to titillate any gathering of dressage ladies with sparkling repartee. By *titillate*, I don't mean literally *titillate*, I mean.....Okay, that's enough of that.

My first piece of advice is try to avoid the kind of sophomoric sexual innuendo that has besmirched this article so far. My next piece of advice, and this is important, so pay attention, is to endeavor to use fancy French words and phrases in your conversation. Not Latin not Spanish, not even Italian. It's French that impresses; it's French that shows you to be the suave **bon viveur** that you know inside that you truly are. Did you notice that when I called you a **bon viveur** it kind of felt good, and you thought, "Yeah, that sounds like me." You see, that's the power of French. If I had called you an effeminate, pretentious glutton, which is basically what it means in English, your reaction might have been somewhat different.

So, French it is. French is the language of romance, the language of culture, the language that the French speak. The French are a wonderful, garlic-intensive people, with great soccer players, and whom God put on this earth to make really good wine. Whenever you interject a French expression into your dialogue, it's best to tilt your head slightly skyward and feel somewhat aloof, in the best Gallic tradition. Incidentally, whenever you describe French wine, never describe it as *really good*, as I just did. That's one of your major **faux pas**, which would cause the French to describe you as **le cretin**. You need to say stuff like, "This impish little wine sports surprising culture and ideal complexity, casually lingering through a persistent finish. Fill me up there, **Pierre**." If descriptions like this don't drip off your tongue, then I suggest writing them on the palm of your hand before the soiree begins, like you used to do before exams at school.

As you are no doubt aware, French words and phrases can be found spread throughout dressage like Cheezwiz on a Ritz. The very word **dressage** is French, meaning to burn money. Then you've got your **Intermediare**, your **Prix St. Georges** and your **pirouettes**. Also there's **renvers, travers, volte, piaffe**.... I could go on, if I knew any more. Actually, there are more, some of them quite obscure, and it's the obscure ones that really impress. Take the expression **chef d'equipe**, who is the manager attached to a dressage team responsible for making all of the practical arrangements, particularly when travelling. Most of your dressage-type folks will know this, but what they probably won't know is how the name originated. Back in 1812, during Napoleon's disastrous retreat from Moscow, the French infantry suffered not just from the bitter cold but also from starvation. The only things they had left that could be considered even slightly edible was their leather equipment, such as their backpacks, straps, webbing, etc. One enterprising corporal named **Emile** (Emily in English) gathered all of his squad's equipment and boiled it in a big pot together with some tree bark, adding a few grams of fresh cilantro and a just a scosch of Basil (who had frozen to death the previous night). All who partook agreed that it tasted **magnifique**, although a few hours later they were all dead of mal d'estomac. Nevertheless **Emile** went down in history as the original **chef d'equipe**, meaning "equipment cook" in English.

Now trot that story out in front of a gathering of well-appointed dressage **connoisseurs** (meaning experts in matters of taste or inveterate snots) and they'll be all over you like marmalade on toast.

The French slang word for a horse is **cheval** (feminine: **la cheval**), named after the famous French entertainer **Maurice Chevalier**, not because he was a horse enthusiast but because, when he laughed, he sounded like a horse. Old **Maurice** was always singing "Tank Evan for Lital Gulls," then he'd laugh "Huh, huh, huh," through his nose, until someone gave him a carrot. The correct French word for horse is **hors**, as in **hors d'oeuvre**, which Archie Bunker used to pronounce "horses' ovaries." Then there is **hors de question** meaning "which horse are you talking about?" and there is **hors de combat** meaning " that big nasty one in the third stall," and **hors de concours** meaning "not the one in the aisle." See if you can work these phrases into any **tête a tête** with a dressage trainer and she will undoubtedly be your bosom buddy or **amie de buste** for life.

Of course, you need not restrict yourself to dressage when impressing your wife's friends with your **repertoire** (meaning repertoire) of French words and phrases. I recommend that you should also pepper your dialogue with French in general, to prove to anyone within earshot that you are a true **boulevardier** (literally, streetwalker). Say, for example, you are discussing the works of Debussy at an upper crust shindig. It would be **apropos** to interject something like "**Debussy** to me has always represented a certain **je ne sais quoi** (meaning damned if I know). His **Claire de Lune** (crazy lady) invokes a sense of **laissez faire** (I could care less), wouldn't you agree?" See if they can top that.

Some other common French phrases that you may find helpful are **terrain vague** (I'm lost again), **temps perdu** (this chicken is cold), **tant pis** (my aunt must excuse herself) and **vive la différence** ("Tank Evan for Lital Gulls").

You must be careful, however, that you don't use a French term in the wrong context, which is a definite **non-non**. For example, you should avoid any phrase that uses the word **femme** (literally Sheila in Australian). **Femme de ménage** does not mean "That woman should be in a zoo" and **femme covert** does not mean "Check out that babe over there." **Cherchez la femme** doesn't mean "Chasing the ladies," although it sounds like it should. It means," A woman must be responsible for this mess," so I'd keep clear of that one if you want to avoid a **slappez de la bouche**.

I hope this has helped my fellow dressage spouses. Unfortunately, I must stop now, because I have to return this French phrase book to the library before I get myself into deep **doux doux**.

Passing the Time at a Dressage Show
The devil makes work for idle hands

Dressage spouses often accompany their wives to shows to provide moral support, maybe to help fetch and carry or because, like me, they have nothing better to do. If you are one of these unfortunates, then you don't need me to tell you that once you have seen a few dressage rides then basically you have seen them all.

Now I know that makes me sound like a total Philistine, but even though I must have watched hundreds of dressage rides, I still can't watch more than two or three in a row. I have a great admiration for those who can, particularly for the judges who often have to remain totally focused on up to twenty rides at a time. I wonder if they ever let their minds drift to, say, last night's episode of Bay Watch, or to what they would do if they won the lottery. Does the scribe have to give them a little nudge now and then? And when they return from their daydreaming to find that they have missed three rides, do they make up the scores and comments? Of course not, they are much too professional for that. Not me—after watching a couple of rides I saunter off to find a more interesting way to amuse myself. Occasionally, I'll come across another bored dressage spouse wandering around aimlessly or studying a blade of grass. I'm always happy to help other poor dopes like me, so allow me to suggest a few activities that you might like to try to help make the day go faster.

Swapping Ribbons

This bit of fun involves removing the ribbons hanging proudly from one stall and replacing them with those from another stall. You can imagine the look on the face of a top rider when she gets back from the port-a-potty to find her two blues and a red gone, and two yellows and a white in their place. It's best not to hang around for too long because, dressage riders, who are normally fun-loving folk, get exceedingly irate when this happens.

Being Profiled

Try this: don one of those flat caps the Europeans like to wear and wander around the trade booths speaking in a loud German accent. All those in earshot immediately profile you as being either an "O" judge or a famous clinician, over here from Dusseldorf to teach these clumsy American duffers the finer points of horsepersonship, and maybe pick up a few American dollars along the way. They will assume that your name is something like Colonel Gerhard von Clauswitz-Schwung, who has written several prestigious dressage instructional books with names like **We have Ways of Making You Piaffe**. Try to avoid eye contact with the peons, just look important and allow them to display the awe in which they hold you. By the way, have you noticed in a lot of these European dressage books, the author often points out that a particular dressage characteristic has no corresponding word in English? They say stuff like, "The unspoken, deeply spiritual bond between rider and horse that we call luffenduffenglockenwursten has no similar word in English," as if to imply that not only do we dorks not understand the basics of dressage but we don't even have words to describe them. Well, there are sixteen million words in the English language, twenty times more than any other language—that's what makes it so special. So maybe we do have a word for it—maybe you or your translator just don't know what it is.

Knobbling the Competition

This one is fun if you can pull it off, and will help your missus in her quest for the color blue. Find her main competitor and wander over to her stall holding a clipboard (if you have a stethoscope around your neck and a pair of those half spectacles that you peer over, all the better). Tell the competitor that your name is Dr. Jeremy H. Coggins, DVM or Dr. Philip Q. Phalanges, DVM and that you are conducting a routine screening as a service to all the competitors. Ask her to show you her horse's teeth, peer at them intently, then ask her if the horse has been out of the country recently, perhaps to the west bank of the river Nile. Emphasize that the east bank of the Nile is no problem, but you need to know if she crossed over to the west side. When she answers that the horse hasn't been out of New Jersey in his life, try to assess the degree of stress in her voice, then ask her if her horse has had his Anthrax shots. When she answers in the negative, say, "Well I shouldn't worry—your horse looks like he is in good shape, given his advanced years." When she tells you that the horse is only seven, advise her not to be too concerned but, if he were your horse, you would have your vet look at it the minute that you arrived back home. That should send her over the top. Hey, the least you can do is help the one you love reach her full potential as a dressage rider.

Volunteering

Dressage show managers are always looking for volunteers, but be careful with this one because you don't know what you may end up having to do. For example, being a scorer can be very boring, and if you decide to relieve the tedium by changing the judges' comments as I once did, then you can find yourself banned from all the shows in a ten state area *(see the article entitled "A Faux Pas at NEDA Fall")*. Outside of scoring, you can still affect the outcome of the competition by volunteering as a runner. Interrupt your run from the scribe to the scorer with a short stop in the port-a-potty. Once safely locked inside, you can change a one to a four but don't change a one to a seven—that would be too obvious. You can change a five, or even a three, to an eight. Hey look, some poor girl didn't spend all that time and energy to be awarded a lousy three on her shoulder-in, no matter how pathetic it was.

Another fun volunteer position is parking attendant. I did this at one show and found great satisfaction by having all the prestigious cars, your BMWs, your Mercs, your Lexuses (or is it Lexi?) park way at the back of the field, so the occupants had the longest to walk. There is no

greater pleasure than bringing those who rule us down a peg or two when the opportunity arises. Sometimes a driver would ignore my directions and park his Audi as close to the show entrance as he pleased. I then parked all subsequent automobiles around his, and he would return to find his car blocked in by an assortment of KIAs, GEOs, Saturns and Escorts. Such small moments make life worthwhile.

General Mischief

If you have to attend a two or three day show, here is a harmless bit of mischief you can pursue. At the end of the day, when your wife and you have finished a enjoyable dinner at a local eatery, washed down by an acceptable bottle of Chateauneuf-de-Pape, she will probably want to head back to the show ground for night barn. While she's tucking in her pride and joy, you can sneak into the competitive area and change all the letters around in the rings.

Who says dressage shows are boring?

Snippets of Dressage History # VVVXV:
A horse, a horse,
My kingdom for an FEI horse

Bloody thou art, bloody will be thy end.
Shame serves thy life and doth thy death attend.
                    Richard III—William Shakespeare

In days of old, when knights were bold
And dressage was not invented
They'd ride their nags, tell a few gags,
And go home quite contented.
                    Lenny IV—Joe Bob Shakespeare

At the battle of Bosworth Field in 1485, King Richard III of England stood defiantly, sword in hand, as his enemies closed in around him. With his horse slain and the battle lost, Richard called out those famous words: "A horse, a horse, my kingdom for a horse." Or did he? Well actually, no, he didn't, because Shakespeare made that up.

What King Richard actually said was, "Would someone please get me the hell out of here," which basically means the same thing, but it doesn't sound as good. In any event, Richard's plea went ignored and Henry Tudor, Duke of Richmond, strode forward and smote Richard dead as a mackerel. Henry then declared himself King Henry VII (*a.k.a. King Henry the Tightwad*).

"So this is all very fascinating, Brian," you're saying, "but what the dickens does it have to do with dressage, foresooth?" Well, the battle of Bosworth Field and the death of Richard III marked the end of the Wars of the Roses, a particularly nasty string of civil wars that lasted for most of the fifteenth century and is the only major conflict that is known to have been caused by a dressage competition. Cast your mind back to 1399, to the All England Dressage finals where the Duke of Lancaster and his cousin, the Duke of York are competing for the top honors. The chief judge was their nephew, an earlier King Richard, King Richard II (*King Richard the Slightly Effeminate*), with the other judges being King Charles VI of France (*King Charles the Clueless*) and Ivan the Terrible of Russia (*Ivan the Terrible*). When the scores were tallied, the Duke of York had edged out the Duke of Lancaster 72.5% to 72.3%, although it was clear Lancaster had ridden the better test. Lancaster's disappointment turned to fury, however, when he learned that York had bribed Ivan of Russia to trade his vote with King Charles of France in exchange for voting for the Muscovite Knight in the jousting competition that was to follow. (Trading votes in international sporting events has long been a tradition between France and Russia).

As King Richard II was presenting a bouquet of red

roses (used in those days before the advent of ribbons) to the Duke of York as the winner, the Duke of Lancaster rode up, snatched the bouquet away from York and smacked him upside the head with it. King Richard tried to intervene in the ensuing fracas, until Lancaster pulled out his dagger and tattooed a fleur-de-lis on the King's pancreas. Lancaster then declared himself King Henry IV, and everyone agreed that the Wars of the Roses had gotten off to a fine start.

Almost immediately, dressage lost its status as England's most popular sport in favor of a newer and slightly more dangerous sport called "Usurping the King." First, the Lancastrian King would be usurped and supplanted by a Yorkist King, who in turn would be usurped in favor of another Lancastrian King and so on for decades. Usually the life span of a recently usurped King was about three minutes, and the magnates who supported him would be hung, drawn and quartered. This was a particularly gruesome procedure, which would definitely ruin your weekend. Eventually a degree of stability was achieved when King Edward IV usurped the throne and reigned for twenty-two years. Edward IV was also known as *King Edward the Horny* because he suffered from what modern historians call the *Bill Clinton Syndrome*. When he died suddenly, his twelve-year-old son became King and, in order to ensure the boy's safety, the dead King's brother, Richard, Duke of Gloucester, locked him up in the Tower of London, together with his younger brother. Then Richard had both of the boys murdered, and declared himself King Richard III, which is where we started. I hope that you are still awake.

Some modern scholars think history gave Richard III

a bum wrap. Shakespeare, and later Laurence Olivier, depicted him as a hideously deformed hunchback, a murderous black-hearted villain, continuously scheming to consolidate the throne that he had so foully stolen. But remember that Shakespeare wrote in the time of Elizabeth I, and Elizabeth's grandfather was Henry Tudor, (the dude who killed Richard back in the first paragraph). Old Bill Shakespeare was not fool enough to write anything that might question the legitimacy of Elizabeth's right to the throne, even though she came from a long line of usurpers. In those days it was easy to be a kiss-ass when the alternative might be to find yourself with a detached head. Contemporary paintings of Richard show him with a slightly deformed arm, but not a hunched back, although portrait painters of that time were also notorious kiss-asses. The truth can be found in the reports that the French and Spanish Ambassadors sent back to their respective monarchs concerning Richard's physical appearance, and no mention of a hunchback was made. So there is a big fat lie about Richard, right there.

The truth is that Richard tried to help the little people, the serfs, the peasants, the laborers get a square deal, not to mention a square meal. Up to that point in history, nobody had given a rodent's derrière about the little people. They were alive simply to serve their masters, pawns in the chess game of medieval politics, scared into compliance by sharp metal weapons and by the retribution of the Church. Richard's attempts to help the oppressed enraged the merchants and the magnates, uniting them in opposition to him. The magnates in particular were attracted to each other by their hatred of the king, so they stuck together, refusing to be polarized (sorry—I couldn't resist that). So Richard's days were numbered. Granted he was no saint, as he did kill those two princes in the Tower of London, and he also had the Duke of Clarence, another one of his brothers, executed. Oh, yes, I forgot about the fact that he murdered his wife so that he could marry his niece, but hey, everyone has a bad day now and again. When his main sidekick, the Duke of Buckingham, plotted against him, Richard had him drowned in a vat of his own wine, which proves that Richard at least had a sense of humor.

In the two short years of his reign, Richard's most important accomplishment was to reintroduce dressage as a major activity in the realm. He loved to compete, but because of his deformed arm, he tended to pull the reins more on his good arm causing an imbalance in the aids, particularly when he signaled with his legs for the horse to move in a straight line. The result was that the horse's hind legs tracked straight down the arena, while the shoulders were brought slightly in off the track. Richard had unwittingly invented the shoulder-in! His two sons, the Earl of Travers and the Duke of Renvers, later took this movement to the next level of complexity. Richard, being a dressage purist, insisted that no unnatural equine movement be allowed in the arena, regardless of how spectacular it appeared. To ensure this could never occur, during a battle with the French he deliberately sought out and single-handedly slew three famous French knights: the Compte de Courbette, the Duc de Capriole and the Marquis de Croupade, and never were their names mentioned in competitive dressage circles again.

Of all European monarchs, Richard III was the one who most championed the sport of dressage, and history records that, even with his dying breath, he called out for his horse (although you and I know different). So I say let's commission a bloody big statue of him, his sword raised to the heavens, his horse on two legs doing a shoulder-in (is that possible?). And absolutely no hunchback. We will place the statue prominently outside of the Dressage Hall of Fame in Lexington, Kentucky, when it is built. Please send your donations to me, in denominations of $100, $50 and, if you must, a pathetic $20, so together we can set the record straight.

Footnote:
An interesting incident took place during the Wars of the Roses when a heavily armored man jumped from a tree onto an attendant of the Earl of Berkeley riding below. Later the incident was commemorated in the song, "A knight in mail sprang on Berkeley's squire."

Peculiarities of the Sport
Curiouser and curiouser

If you have read any of my incredibly accurate items entitled, *Snippets of Dressage History,* you will be aware that the discipline of dressage has been around since Saint Peter was a cowboy. So it's no surprise that dressage has developed many peculiarities over the centuries. Of course dressage is not alone in this respect, as many sports seem to have peculiarities, some more bizarre than others. In fact, to the true sports fan, the more bizarre the peculiarities, the more interesting the sport, so let's consider a few other sports before we look at the oddities of dressage.

Take curling for example. Curling is one of those sports that surely was invented by a group of guys bombed out of their gourds one night, who decided it would be a blast if they went out onto a frozen lake and hurled large stones across the ice. It's not sliding stones at a target that's particularly peculiar, after all that's just a variation of bowling or darts. No, what is really weird is that two of those dudes were carrying brooms (don't ask me why) and they followed the stone down the ice brushing like crazy. It doesn't get more bizarre than that.

Another sport that clearly falls into the "strange" category is Greco-Roman wrestling. Now I'm not one to criticize a sport, after all I am a dressage fan, but it's hard to imagine any activity, categorized as a sport, that brings two guys as close together as that one does. Except maybe the two-man luge. Not that there is anything wrong with that, you understand. Speaking of wrestling, there is one form of that sport that I will go out of my way to watch, and that is Sumo wrestling. Who thought this one up? Two obscenely obese Japanese guys, wearing nothing but tiny thongs, trying to push each other out of a small ring. Brilliant! I could watch it all night. You've really got to love those wacky Japanese.

The world's favorite sport is soccer and rightly so. A wonderful peculiarity of men's soccer occurs when a free kick is awarded just outside the penalty area and several players stand shoulder to shoulder in front of the kicker to form a human wall. The idea is to block the ball with their bodies, but there is one particular part of their body that they would prefer did not take part in this tactic, so they hold their hands over their "particulars." You may have seen this—it tends to make women howl with laughter. These guys would prefer to take a soccer ball full in the face travelling at fifty miles an hour than to have any harm come to the family jewels. Nothing better illustrates the priorities of the human male.

Another really strange, not to mention gross, tradition of soccer is the swapping of jerseys at the end of an international match. Playing for your country against another country is considered a great honor so many players commemorate the occasion by collecting the jerseys of their opponents. Two opposing players will remove their jersey at the end of the game, swap them, and then put on the other player's jersey! Honest. These guys have just finished ninety minutes of grueling soccer action and are sweating like stuffed pigs, then they take some stranger's reeking, perspiration-soaked jersey and put it on. To be honest, I never realized just how disgusting this practice is until my wife pointed it out to me, which gives you some idea where hygiene sits in my list of priorities.

Now, let's consider some of the peculiarities associated with dressage. The first one that comes to mind is the judging. There cannot be any other sport where the contestants are given a score out of ten, accompanied in most cases by written feedback for *every single movement the horse makes during the test*! The rider receives three full pages of scores together with an explanation of why a particular score was given, plus a summary of the overall ride and suggestions for improvement. That is truly incredible, and the sport of dressage should be proud of this process. This method should be adopted by every sport that requires subjective judgement for scoring, particularly the sport of ice skating whose judging process is more corrupt than a church full of medieval popes.

On the other hand, one of the aspects of ice skating that could be adopted by dressage is the dress code. Dressage riders all dress alike—how boring is that? Not that the outfit isn't very classic and elegant, it's just that the same outfit every time adds a touch of tedium to what is otherwise a white-hot exciting experience for the spectator. The only deviation in the dress code is that if you are in the military or in the police, you are allowed to wear your uniform. Not to detract from these two honorable professions, but why are they considered special enough to wear their day clothes? Why not let, say, an airline pilot wear her uniform, or an accountant wear her business suit, a Playboy bunny wear her birthday suit, a middle manager wear business casual (at least on Fridays). The problem with allowing everyone to wear their work clothes I suppose is that, whereas the Adult Amateurs would all be dressed differently, the Pros would all be dressed in smelly old blue jeans and horse stained tee shirts that have written on them something like, "To ride or not to ride? What a stupid question."

Okay, so wearing your work clothes isn't such a good idea. So, I say let's just allow the rider to wear any outfit that matches her mood or tickles her fancy or at least reflects her freestyle music. Male riders could pick one of those outfits that the Village People used to wear. I know, I know, dressage is a serious and classical equine discipline that celebrates the harmony of horse and rider, in which there is no place for levity blah, blah, blah, blah, blah. Look, I'm just trying to add a little variety to attract more spectators. I'm certainly not suggesting that riders adopt those skimpy, provocative dresses female ice skaters wear. Okay, maybe I am.

While we are on the subject of dress, the dressage outfit needs to be not only smart but also clean. Yet dressage has a lot of dirt associated with it. There is always a lot of horse slobber flying around, and often mud splashing up from the ring, particularly after a rain shower. If it's hot and dry, there are clouds of dust to be ridden through.

Horse manure lies everywhere, puddles and potholes abound. Probably the only sport in which females participate that is dirtier is mud-wrestling. Now there's a classy sport for you.

Another peculiarity of dressage is the training that goes on in the warm up area before a rider goes in for the test. You have a trainer barking out instructions to his pupil, just a few minutes before she enters the ring. Isn't it a bit late to be training at that point? Is the rider going to say, "Oh now I get it—why didn't you say that earlier?" Words of encouragement are fine, but actual training, I would think, would be a distraction. But, hey, what do I know?

The first dressage competition that I attended was the World Cup in Toronto, about sixteen years ago (it's been downhill since then). My wife, Sue, and I had recently become an item and I think she was hoping that I would be impressed by her sport, so the World Cup was the best place to start. And impressed I was, particularly by how every aspect of the event seemed so refined: the riding, the spectators, the food, the portable toilets. I found myself in a stratum of society a little higher than I was used to, among people who pay about $20 more for a bottle of wine, and who probably sport an extra zero on their annual incomes. Still, I enjoyed the competition. Thousands of spectators watched in appreciative silence as the world's top riders performed their equestrian magic. At the end of a ride, polite applause rippled through the audience, and naturally I joined in, although I didn't have a clue what I was clapping for. Then the announcer, who had a snooty British accent and a hyphenated surname, as they often do (incidentally, these accents can be purchased in New Jersey—that's where I got mine), informed everyone that applause must be held until the rider had left the ring. I couldn't believe it! Not only is it a faux pas to applaud during the test but also at the end of the test—you have to wait until the rider has left the ring! What type of affected elitism is this, I asked myself? Do you know of any other sport that requires the athlete to leave the arena before the spectators can show their appreciation?

A few years later, having learned enough about dressage to appreciate a good ride, and having become an affected elitist myself, I witnessed Robert Dover ride an exhibition freestyle at the Washington Horse Show that was one of the most beautiful spectacles I had ever seen. As captivating as it was, I still waited until the end of the ride before I exploded in noisy appreciation, because, after all, I didn't want anyone around me to know that I was genetically programmed to be a soccer hooligan. So, my point is, if a rider performs an excellent movement during a test at any level, why not let the spectators show their approval at the time the movement is made? The judges are much too professional to be influenced by a crowd, and the rider will surely appreciate it, particularly if the rider is an amateur. I'm not suggesting that people yell, "You go, Girl," or, "Kick some serious ass, Betsy," but would it really be gauche to show a little appreciation for an excellent movement or a seamless transition? And maybe at the end of the class, the competitors could gather around the ring to allow the spectators to give them the clap that they so richly deserve.

Don't get the wrong idea. I'm not advocating that dressage drastically change its customs or structure, nor am I suggesting that dressage adopt many characteristics of other sports. There are some that just would not be good for dressage. Like instant replay, for example. Can you imagine interrupting the frantic excitement of a dressage test to allow the judges to peer into a replay camera to check if the angle of the travers was 30 degrees in the direction of the movement? I hardly think so. Nor is their anything in baseball that would easily transfer over to dressage. Can you imagine a renowned trainer, who disagrees with a judge's scoring, running over to the judge's box and kicking sand over the judge's pumps? Actually, I *can* imagine that and it sounds like fun, but it will not do, my friends, it will not stand. Can you imagine judges, trainers and riders alike hocking one up and spitting on the ring every few seconds, or performing an inventory on their naughty bits every couple of minutes? That one I can't imagine—neither do I want to. I always find it a mild source of amusement when watching a baseball game on TV when some jock, getting paid $24 million dollars a year, starts spitting in close up and scratching himself in front of millions of viewers. I guess money can't buy class. But hey, that's just another peculiarity of sports, so I'm all for it. Now, go out and buy one of those skimpy ice skaters' costumes!

The Ten Commandments of Dressage
Holy Moses, follows these rules religiously

1.   Thou shalt have no other passion than dressage.

2.   Thou shalt not set thyself up as an expert unless
      thou knowest what the hell thou art talking about.

3.   Thou shalt not take the name of thy judges in vain.

4.   Six days shalt thou train, but for heaven's sake
      give it a rest on Monday.

5.   Thou shalt not kill thy groom, even if she braideth
      like a deranged amputee on angel dust.

6.   Honor thy local dressage association volunteers.

7.   Thou shalt not forsake thy spouse every weekend
      of the show season. Thou needeth to understand
      the importance of this commandment.

8. Thou shalt not steal thy neighbor's muck bucket.

9. Thou shalt not fib about how many were in the class when thou winneth a ribbon.

10. Thou shalt not covet thy neighbor's tack box, nor her freestyle music, nor her fancy grooming thingy.

A Hat in the Ring: A Love Story
A dressage princess
and a stable boy proceed at the trot

Her eyes they shone like the diamonds
He thought her the Queen of the Land
And her hair it hung over her shoulders
Tied up with a black velvet band.

Old Irish Ballad

It was in the month of August 1957 at Witherspoon Farm , N.J., when young Danny O'Boyle first spied the lovely Penelope. Smitten he was, smitten such that for once he was lost for words. He just stared at her, as she buckled the bridle on her horse's head no more than three stalls away from where he stood.

"Did you never learn that it is very rude to stare," she asked, in a voice cultured by the best education that money could buy. Danny did not answer her taunt, he just continued to stare and smile.

"Maybe the boy does not speak English," jibed Penelope's trainer, the inimitable Charlotte Witherspoon. "You are not being paid to leer at our clients, young man. You are being paid to muck out the stalls, and I suggest that's what you continue to do, if you want to stay employed. Nod if you understand me."

Danny ignored the older woman, "Your forgiveness, please, young lady, but I mistook you for Audrey Hepburn and now I see my mistake. You are younger and much prettier."

Penelope smiled, "Would you listen to his sass, Charlotte. Where are you getting your help from these days? Who performs the interviews?"

"And what would you have me do?" answered Danny, warming to the repartee, "Hold my tongue and let the moment pass? Ah no, I'd regret it the rest of my days. I wouldn't miss the chance to say hello before John Ford whisks you off the Hollywood."

Penelope mounted her horse. "Time for my lesson—I have to go," she turned and looked back down at Danny, "You have a twinkle in your eye, stable boy, so I think you may be a rascal," she smiled again.

"I'm sorry about that," Charlotte huffed to Penelope as she led Penelope's horse into the indoor arena. "I'll fire him as soon as your lesson is over."

"No you won't" Penelope answered, "No you won't."

Mary O'Boyle heard the key in the latch, "Is that you, Danny?" she yelled.

Danny burst through the door, skipped down the hall and into the kitchen. He threw his arms around his mother's large midriff, as she stood at the sink washing dishes, and kissed her hard on the back of her neck.

"Mary, mother of God, you scared the beJesus out of me!" she yelped. "What in Hades has gotten into you?"

Danny pulled over a chair, lent back on it and sprawled his feet up on the kitchen table.

"You know, Ma, here's the question I'm struggling with. How come I'm blessed with the best mother on earth? Why—I ask myself—why did I have the great fortune to be born to unarguably, indisputably, irrevocably, the best damn woman ever to bear the exalted title of mother? If ever there were an Olympic event for being a mother, you'd be there on the podium, all gilded and smiling, waving the Irish flag on high. My Ma, the World Champion."

"Ah shut yer gob, you great big dollop of lard," came the response. "What's come over yer? What happened to you today to make you king of the world?"

"Today, Ma ... today I met a wonderful girl. Her name is Penelope. The Goddess Penelope, Princess Penelope, The Marchioness Penelope, La Contessa Penelope, Mademoiselle Penelope, Her Royal Loveliness Pen…."

"Ah shut yer cake hole, yer daft cabbage," his mother interrupted, " How many girls did you meet today, for God's sake? So tell me about her, this Penelope. What sort of a name is that anyway? Sounds like a money name to me."

"Ah Ma, you wouldn't believe it. She is just beautiful. Spittin' image of Audrey Hepburn in Roman Holiday, skin as smooth as Merle Oberon in The Scarlet Pimpernel, a smile that Maureen O'Hara would be proud of in The Quiet Man. Penelope could star in any movie."

"Bride of Frankenstein, perhaps?"

"And her hair," continued Danny, "defies description. It flows like a cascade in slow motion down her back."

"None on her head—just down her back?"

"Enough, mother, enough. I'll have you take this seriously. I have found my Helen, my Aphrodite, my Eleanor of Aquitaine, my Lizzie Borden."

"Your Lizzie Borden?"

"Just seeing if you were paying attention."

"And does she feel the same way about you?"

"Not now, Ma, she's in love with a horse. But she will...she will. Penelope is a young dressage rider—a rider in training—a woman in training. Her leather britches cling to her gorgeous young thighs, her white blouse engulf her exquisite...."

"Enough of that, me lad. There'll be no talk like that in this house," she shook her finger at him. "Ah, I knew she was money. Horses like that spell money, and you—what are you? You don't have two cents to rub together and you're wooing an heiress for pity's sake. And pity is all you'll probably get from her and her family. Look at you—you shovel horse muck fer a livin'. Why should she look at the likes of you? Go back to school, Danny, make something of yerself. Your father, God rest his soul, didn't bring us all the way to America for you to be shoveling horse manure. My God, you could have done that back in Ireland and saved us the cost of the passage!"

"I've told you before, Ma, it's all part of the plan. I'm gaining experience, drinking in the blessed knowledge of life. From job to job I go, a little bit richer in the ways of the world each time, and when the big opportunity comes my way I'll be more than ready. All these jobs are just preparation for when our ship comes in, then I'll jump on it like a flea on a dog, and Penelope and I will sail off into the sunset of everlasting bliss."

"And me — what will become of yer old Ma?"

"Ma, I'll be a millionaire many times over and I'll give half to you, I promise."

"I'll settle for one tenth."

"I'll give you a third, and that's my final offer—take it or leave it."

"You drive a hard bargain, Danny O'Boyle."

The next morning, Danny was back at work, heaving bags of shavings up in the hayloft, when up the steps came Penelope.

"Look I'm sorry about yesterday," she smiled, "We were rude—I was rude."

Danny smiled back, "Sure I was leerin' at you like a big gorp. It's me that should apologize. My name is Danny, Danny O'Boyle."

"I know," she said. "I asked."

"Would you like to go out with me sometime? Say, tonight for example."

"You waste no time, Danny. Yes, I think that would be fine. Where shall we go?"

"I'll have my man pick you up in the Bentley, then we'll charter a private plane to the Riviera. I have a little chateau there, you know. We'll dine on the terrace, watching the moon come up over the Cote d'Azur, sipping 100-year-old Cognac, and we'll be back before they notice that we were gone."

"How about the drive-in?"

"Perfect."

Their eyes locked for a brief moment, caught in the force that had caused the species to perpetuate for a million years, involuntarily reacting to ancient genes that control the attraction of the sexes. Then she turned around, walked towards the steps, stopped and turned back to Danny. She lolled her head on one side and asked sweetly, "Would you like to kiss me?"

Danny was startled by the question, by its naivete, by its innocence. "Is the Pope Catholic?" he grinned. Danny kissed her softly, like Bogie kissed Ingrid Bergman in Casablanca, liked Randolph Scott kissed Grace Kelly in High Noon. Suddenly the moment was shattered by the overwhelming presence of Charlotte Witherspoon hovering behind them.

"What's going on here," she shrieked. "Just what do you two think that you're up to. I'll have none of this in my barn, and don't think that I won't tell your parents about this, Penelope. Just two months ago you were a minor—this is almost illegal." She turned to Danny, "And as for you, you riff-raff, you are fired. Get your stuff and leave right my property right now."

"It was only a kiss, for heavens sake," said Penelope.

"I wish you no trouble," said Danny, turning to leave. "I'll be on my way, but I'll still see you later I hope," winking at Penelope as he left. Stopping briefly at Charlotte, he whispered, "You know, you ought to be ashamed of yourself, making a frail young girl like that dig for coal."

"What?" she asked, "What?"

"You said that she was a miner," Danny smiled.

"Get out," said Charlotte.

The next day, Danny bounded down the stairs and into the kitchen. "Mornin', Ma. How's my wonderful mother this fine mornin'? I know what you're going to ask—why am I not at work? Well, I'm fired, that's why, but no matter."

"What else is new?" his mother replied, pouring him a cup of coffee. "And how was yer date last night?"

"Ah, Ma, I'm glad you asked. It was simply grand. There's an indefinable attraction between Penelope and me. We went to the drive-in and saw Ingrid Berman in Anastasia. Ah, but that Ingrid Berman is a beautiful woman, but she can't hold a candle to Penelope. We yaked and yaked like a couple of lovelorn kids—which I suppose is what we are. You know, you were right, her family is rich, but I'm not going to hold that against her. She loves her horse, some type of Fresian or something, and she loves to ride in dressage competitions. In fact she's riding in a big show next week, where she'll be moving up into the International Classes, riding something called Prix St. Georges. Now, doesn't that sound fancy? She has to buy new riding clothes for these higher classes, like a long black coat with tails, and one of those quaint little top hats. She'll look like the Queen of Monrovia. Now, let me ask you, can you believe my good fortune in meeting someone like Penelope?"

"I'm glad for yer, Danny—I really am" said his mother, joining him at the kitchen table, "but I don't want yer gettin' too close to a girl like this. She'll string you along for a while, just for fun, and then she'll be off to some fancy college leavin' yer with a broken heart. I'm just afraid that someday some girl will take that lilt from yer voice, that twinkle from yer eye, that joy out of yer soul. I want to be long in me grave when that happens. Just be careful, son, that's all."

Danny felt a little out of place when he entered the store with the fancy title, Equine Sports Equipment Emporium. He approached a somewhat stern looking woman behind the counter.

"I'm looking to buy one of those fancy little top hats that dressage riders wear," he smiled.

"What size?" she asked coldly.

"Well it's for a young lady, and I'm not sure of the size. But her head is the cutest thing that you ever did see, and it's smaller than, say, Ava Gardner but not as small as Judy Garland."

The woman remained expressionless, "About this size?" she asked, producing a hat. "That will be $57."
Danny laughed, "I'm not wanting to buy shares in your store."

"The price is $57," came the steely response.

"But I only have $35 to my name," Danny pleaded. "Can I pay it in six easy installments—or maybe three hard ones?"

"We don't do that sort of thing," she replied haughtily.

"Well, here is $35 on deposit. I'll be back quicker than a startled rabbit."

Liam McHugh, the Pawnbroker, bowed his head and looked over his glasses at Danny O'Boyle. "I'll give yer $5 fer the genuine fake wrist watch and $17 fer the guitar, me lad," he said.

"It's a sign," cried Danny, "a sign from heaven—$22 is the exact amount I need!"

Twenty minutes later, Danny was back in the Equine equipment store. "It's me again," smiled Danny to the sour shop lady, plopping a wad of banknotes on the counter, "Here is the rest—that makes $57 in al.l"

She didn't touch the money. "Plus tax," she sneered.

"Plus tax?" cried Danny. "You didn't mention the tax before. I have no more money!"

"Plus tax," she looked at him like he was a complete idiot.

The two glowered at each other for a good ten seconds before Danny broke the silence.

"As upset as I am by this unfortunate turn of events," he sighed, "I feel compelled to mention that when the sun streams through the shop window and bathes the side of your face like that, you are the spittin' image of Rita Hayward—but I expect that you've heard that many times before."

She continued to glower at him, until gradually her tight lips broke into a smile. "Take the damn hat," she said.

"Pssst...Pssst, Penelope—over here," hissed Danny, as he furtively peered around the side of the barn.

"What are you doing here?" whispered Penelope, "If Charlotte sees you, she'll call the police."

"No matter," said Danny. "Here, I have a present for you," and handed her a large gift box.

Opening the box, she cried, "Why it's a dressage hat! And I've haven't bought one yet. Danny, Danny it's beautiful. You shouldn't have—they are so expensive."

Excitedly, she tried on the hat, "I wish I had a mirror handy. Wait, It's a little bit big," she said jiggling it on her head. Danny looked inside the hat, "I think just a little bit of material glued to the inside will do the trick, I'll take it home and fix it."

"Here use this." She untied the black ribbon of velvet that held up her long sleek hair and gave it to him.

There were plenty of spectators on hand for the dressage show. After the morning rain, the competitors and their trainers were practicing for their forthcoming tests in the early afternoon sun. Danny mingled with the crowd, hoping not to be noticed, until it was Penelope's turn to ride and then he moved close to the dressage arena. Inevitably, he bumped into Charlotte Witherspoon.

"What are you doing, here?" she demanded. "If you continue to harass this girl, I'm going to report you to the authorities. Don't you understand—you're not in her class!"

"This show is open to the public. So here I stay."

The confrontation was cut short, as their attentions turned to Penelope about to enter the ring. Charlotte walked over and began talking to a man and a woman, exclusive-looking people whom Danny surmised must be Penelope's parents. She pointed at Penelope, and then swung around to point at Danny, bringing their attention on him. Danny waved.

The judges' whistle blew and Penelope entered the ring. "Ah, what a magnificent sight she is," thought Danny. She was all dressed in black and white, shining boots, twinkling brass and gold, tiny white-gloved hands gripping leather, steering the great beast around the arena. Her horse was black polished muscle, alert and feisty, ready to respond, muzzle frothing, controlled to the edge by a slip of a girl. They glided through the movements like they were riding on a magic carpet.

Then suddenly, as they broke into a canter, Penelope's hat flew off! It landed rim side down in the mud, just a few feet away from the corner of the ring. As Penelope continued with her test, Danny stared at the hat in apprehension. "Oh no," he thought, "What will happen when they come around again? The horse might spook at the hat—it might throw her! Or it might step on the hat and grind it into the mud. That hat cost me $57!"

While the horse was at the far end of the ring, Danny quickly jumped into the ring, grabbed the hat and jumped out again. Suddenly the whistle blew twice. Danny stopped in his tracks. Penelope had stopped her test and was talking to one of the judges. Everyone was staring at Danny, the other judges, the spectators, Penelope's parents, Charlotte—everyone. "Oh no, what have I done," he thought.

Charlotte strode over to him, black fury on her face. "What the hell did you do that for?" She yelled at him. "It's an automatic disqualification when someone enters the ring, you idiot! She was acing that test, at least 65%; she would have qualified for the regional finals. She had the blue ribbon sewn up."

"I'm sorry—I'm really sorry," he sputtered.

Charlotte's venom continued to spill out, "Do you have any concept of how much training, how much work it takes to reach this point, how many years are involved? And money? How much money do you think her parents must have spent to get their daughter to this point? You are not saying much now, are you? No fancy talk, no sarcasm now, you stupid boy!" Charlotte stomped away.

Danny looked over at Penelope, dismounted now, out of the ring and talking to her parents. He stood dejected, his chin on his chest, still gripping the offending hat. She's right, he thought, I am an idiot. I've ruined everything. I've killed it before it had chance to get started. He began to walk away when he felt a tap on his shoulder. It was Penelope.

"I don't know what to…" he began.

"Then don't say anything," she said. "Can I have my hat back?"

116

He held out the hat towards her, but instead of taking the hat she took hold of his wrist, pulled him towards her, and kissed him gently on his cheek.

"There will be other shows, other tests," she whispered. Then she turned and walked away. After a few steps, she stopped and turned around.

"By the way", she smiled, " My parents are wondering if you would like to come to dinner tonight?"

Snippets of Dressage History # LLLDI:
Dick Turpin's last ride

If you are an American person, then you may not have heard of the legendary highwayman Dick Turpin and his famous ride from London to York. The story of Dick Turpin and his magnificent mare, Black Bess, is as familiar in Britain as Paul Revere's famous ride is in America (*see Snippet No. XIVCDI: Paul Revere's Big Night Out*). What is generally not known however is that Dick Turpin, like Paul Revere, was an early proponent of the wonderful sport of dressage.

Dick and Black Bess entered all of the major dressage events in Southern England during the early eighteenth century. Being both English and a dressage rider, Dick surprisingly wasn't gay. In fact, with his dark good looks and his innate charm, Dick was a big hit with the lady riders. Some called him a bon vivant and some called him a boulevardier, the other male rider called him a lucky bastard. But Dick's happy-go-lucky, devil-may-care demeanor masked an ugly flaw in his character—he had a wicked bad temper. It was his temper that led him on the road to out-lawry, a road that ended on the scaffold at York racecourse.

Dick's misfortunes began right in the middle of a dressage test, Adult Amateur Fourth Level, when a large R judge at C marked Dick low on a double coefficient movement that Dick thought approached perfection. Dick's temper flared and, pulling out his pistol, he shot the judge right in the judge's box. Clutching his chest, the judge staggered over to G, pirouetted past D and fell dead at X. Everyone saluted. Now you may ask yourself, "Why would a Dressage rider carry a pistol during a test?" Well in those days, soccer had not yet been invented so all the hooligans attended the next most exciting sporting event—dressage shows. Competitors found it prudent to carry a firearm in case the crowd became unruly. Of course nowadays if you enter the ring with a .38 Smith and Wesson sticking out of your britches, you are bound to be marked low. Well, maybe not in Texas. Anyway, back to Dick and his predicament. Although all of the other competitors agreed that the incident was justifiable homicide, they couldn't be sure that the local magistrate would agree, so they advised Dick to make a run for it and spend the rest of his life hunted like a dog.

Holed up in Epping Forest, east of London, Dick Turpin donned the role of a masked Highwayman and a legend was born. Holding up stagecoaches in the countryside in the most gentlemanly manner, Dick would doff his hat to the menfolk and kiss the ladies' hands as he removed their jewelry. He was so charming that gentlefolk didn't really mind being robbed by him, and it became quite the status symbol amongst the aristocracy to be his victim. Occasionally Dick would kidnap a young lady from the

stagecoach in order to teach her the finer points of dressage, but he would always return her within the hour, somewhat flushed, yet none the worse for wear. In fact, hoping for one of Dick's famous dressage lessons, many young ladies would wander the roads at night in the off chance he might kidnap them. As Dick grew richer, the price on his head grew larger. Eventually he teamed up with another highwayman, the debonair "Captain" Tom King, and together the gallant pair of swashbucklers raided far and wide. Then one fateful night in the forest, Dick and Tom got into a heated discussion regarding dressage training methods. Dick favored the controversial "long, low, and deep" way of riding, arguing that it can help to promote maximum development of looseness, maintenance of a healthy locomotion system, and optimum psychological health in the horse (as opposed to the rider). Tom strongly disagreed. So Dick pulled out his pistol and shot Tom deader than a sausage. There was that famous temper again.

With a heavy heart, Dick Turpin and Black Bess gave up the highwayman's life. The fugitives settled down in York, in the north of England, Dick changing his name to John Palmer and Black Bess changing her name to Dobbin, living the life of the landed gentry. Although Dick still financed his fancy lifestyle with the occasional highway robbery, he longed for one last big heist to set him up for life, so he traveled back to London and robbed the King's Mail coach. Pursued by an entire regiment of the King's Dragoon Guards, Dick and Black Bess began their legendary non-stop ride back to York, two hundred miles to the north. Throughout the day and night they rode, over streams, fields, hills, dales, deserts, tundra, glacial formations. The common folk came out to cheer them on. Centuries later, locals would point to Black Bess's hoof prints on gates still remaining after the legendary ride. The pair arrived at York in time to take part in a local dressage show, thereby creating their alibi, as all believed that it was impossible to commit a robbery in London and just two days later enter a dressage competition in York. Unfortunately the technical director at the show was the self same technical director at the London show were Dick had shot the judge years before. Dick was arrested, found guilty and sentenced to death. After the fourth race at York racecourse, a scaffold was erected, a hanging being the usual method of entertaining the race-going crowd between races.

With his hands tied behind his back, Dick was placed on the back of Black Bess and the noose put over his neck.

Then the executioner gave the horse a sharp slap on the rump-yet Black Bess did not move. A guard held up a carrot in front of her nose to try and coax her forward, but she remained steadfast. Then two men whipped her smartly on either flank—and still she would not move. "Cease this cruelty!" yelled Dick, then quietly he whispered to his horse, "You have done all you can, old girl. We'll meet again in sweeter pastures." Dick gave her the command with his legs and Black Bess transitioned from the halt to the trot, then to the canter, disappearing into the early evening mist, never to be seen again.

Riding to Perfection:
Tips and techniques from an expert

After watching so many dressage tests and witnessing so many training sessions in my exalted position as chief cheerleader for my wife, I am bound to have amassed a mountain of information on how to ride perfectly at every level. In fact, all this dressage stuff occupies far too much space in my feeble excuse for a brain—space that I could use for more important things, like remembering where I left my car keys or the names of the Liverpool soccer team that won the European Cup in 1981. Just in preparing this book I have committed to memory much more dressage stuff than I will ever want or need.

So I've decided to do a dressage data dump, and share with you this mass of information at no charge, saving you vast amounts of time and money in training sessions, clinics, books and magazines. We'll start with a short but pompous evaluation of what constitutes a perfect ride, then deal specifically with the basics, finally transitioning elegantly into the upper levels. Are you saddled up? Then let's proceed.

The Essence of Perfect Riding

Every dressage expert seems to have his or her own definition of what constitutes perfect horsepersonship. Some say it's mental and physical control; some say it's a combination of balance and suppleness; others are convinced it's harmony and trust. Personally, I believe that dressage excellence is 50% knowledge, 50% confidence and 50% arithmetic, but what do I know?. Actually, what I do know is that if you laid all of the dressage experts end-to-end from here to Germany, many of them would drown in the North Atlantic.

You will hear some experts say dressage is a very difficult sport to master, and others say that riders tend to make dressage more complicated than it really is. These latter experts maintain that it is easier to become adept in this sport than is commonly believed and, if you ensure that your basics are solid before you move on, everything else will fall into place. To these experts I say, "Kiss my martingales—who are you trying to kid?" Everything about dressage is difficult regardless of how many years you spend working on the basics. There is not one easy aspect to it—nothing is intuitive, nothing will fall into place, and nothing is second nature. You can go over to Holland or Germany and buy yourself a $250,000 Grand Prix horse, bring him home, hire the best trainers and you will still find Training Level, Test 1 much harder than, say, trying to program a VCR. Hey, if it was easy, anyone could do it.

I'm not suggesting that the basics are unimportant. You have to learn to swim before you enter the Olympic 500-meter butterfly, unless you use a lot of steroids. So let us examine some dressage basics, shall we, starting with:

The Seat

A firm position in the middle part of the horse is essential. Sit on the horse's head and you will fall off when he bends his head down; sit on his rump and you will slide off his back. Judges will deduct marks in both cases. Your two seat bones and your crotch (pardon my French) should form a triangle or, if you are overweight, a parallelogram. From your seat you will influence your horse by contracting or relaxing your loin muscle. If you don't know where your loin muscle is or, in fact, what it is, then locate a Bible with illustrations and turn to the page where Samson girds his loins. Thus you will find your loin muscle is in your groin area, and a groin injury can result if you contract your loin muscle too often (see **Common Dressage Ailments**). Keep your thighs and knees flat against the saddle, your kneecaps pointing forward. If your kneecaps point backwards, a groin injury is the least of your worries. Your feet should be parallel to the horse, one on each side.

The Aids

Aids are the signals by which the rider conveys her wishes to the horse, and are divided into natural and artificial as follows:

Natural aids: Voice, legs, hands, knees, bumps-a-daisy, ginseng, green tea.

Artificial aids: Whips, spurs, sugar lumps, Saran wrap, Viagra, gin and tonic.

The leg aids are the most difficult to learn, but they are also the most important, and once mastered it will appear to the onlooker that the rider need only think of a command and the horse will obey. Zorro and Tornado communicated that way all the time, as did Roy and Trigger. How does it work then, this wonderful kind of human to horse ESP?

It starts with a need for you to perform a certain movement, say halt at X, which is generated in that part of your brain known as the cerebral processing unit or CPU. The CPU pulls the halt movement from your memory banks located in your upper left cranium region, processes it and creates a signal called a synapse (or canapé if you are French). A synapse is an electrical impulse of about 100 gigavolts but lasts for only one nanozillionth of a second, which is just as well. This electrical impulse shoots down your spine like a dose of salts, takes a left at your spleen, fakes out your colon, and splits into two at your small intestines. One part goes down one leg, the other down the other leg, until they reach your calf muscles, causing them to twitch. This twitching excites the molecules of your leather boots, which in turn excites that part of the saddle that your boots are pressed against. (Other excitement caused by leather boots is covered in a later chapter).

Molecular agitation continues right through the saddle into your horse's flanks, creating another small, but now equine, electrical charge known as a volte. This charge shoots up your horse's haunches, bypassing his withers, poll and fetlock until it reaches his brain, which is about the size of an avocado pit, located in his head area. When the horse receives this message, he mistakes it for a fly and swats it with his tail. No, he draws data from his own memory bank that says that the rider wants to halt, so he sends four identical signals to his legs to tell them to quit moving. This whole process takes about twenty minutes, by which time the show is over and the judges have gone home. So the important lesson here is to anticipate the movement well in advance. On the other hand, you could just say "whoa" and the horse would halt, but in dressage, of course, that is against the rules.

The Half Halt

As the name implies, this movement occurs when one half of the horse/rider combination halts, and the other half doesn't. It is particularly common among inexperienced dressage riders when they inadvertently give a cantering horse the signal to halt. The horse comes to a screeching stop and the rider continues over the horse's head. Although this exciting movement is very popular with the spectators, the judges tend to frown on it and marks will be deducted.

The Counter Canter

The right lead on the right rein is called the true canter, and the left lead on the left rein is also called the true canter. The left lead on the right rein is called the counter canter and, if the horse picks up the right lead on the left rein, I have no idea what it is called. It is essential, however, that you put your right lead in, then your right lead out, in, out, in, out, pirouette about, do the counter canter and turn yourself around. That's basically what it's all about.

Transitions

During the transitions, you must always ensure the purity and evenness of the gaits. That's all that I'm going to say on that particular subject.

Flying Changes

This is the very devil of a movement to master. I noticed when my wife was teaching her younger horse this movement what seemed to help the most was for her to curse almost the entire time. In fact, she invented some new words that would make a sailor blush, yelling so loudly that she could be heard three towns over, which is perhaps why our neighbors don't speak to us anymore. Still, I think the horse sensed she wasn't happy with him. So you might try adding cursing to your repertoire of natural aids although, by this stage, you probably already have.

Flying changes are difficult because the rider has to communicate aids from the seat, legs, hands and shoulders virtually simultaneously as the horse is in mid-stride. The horse must be sensitive enough to recognize these aids and adjust his legs immediately. This process in German is called *Durclangenhorsanblitzen* (with two little dots over the 'a's), but there is no equivalent word in English. Unfortunately, I don't speak German so I can't help you any further. But my advice is this: if you continue to experience difficulty in mastering flying changes, then sell the damn horse and get another one. Look, life is too short for you to be spending all of your time and money on an animal that can't even learn how to skip. It's got four legs, for crying out loud—how hard can it be?

The Limbo

There is no dressage movement called the Limbo—I was just seeing if you were paying attention.

The Canter Pirouette

This extremely difficult upper level movement requires complex techniques, a high degree of collection, and precise balance. If I were you, I wouldn't even attempt it, except for the fact that it's included in the tests, where it's designed to separate the women from the girls. Often, canter pirouettes that you will witness at dressage shows are so choppy they look like Charlie Chaplin doing a U-turn (except for my wife's rides of course, where she performs the movement perfectly, as indeed she does with everything else in life that she attempts).

The search for a flawless canter pirouette can be a frustrating experience, but there are certain tactics you can employ that are used by many of your top riders.

In Europe, for example, your Germans, your Dutch, your French, your Liechtensteiners start by riding around in circles, gradually decreasing the size of the circle until they perform a perfect pirouette, or until horse and rider get so dizzy that they fall over. This technique is much easier to perform in Europe than in the States because there is so little space in most European countries that people are used to turning around in small circles. American riders, however, can use those little horsie carousels that you sometimes find outside of Wal-Mart to practice riding in small circles. Just be sure that you don't see anyone that you know.

Another technique used by trainers to elicit an excellent canter pirouette is to have the rider canter away and then yell, "HEY, LOOK WHO'S HERE—IT'S TOM CRUISE!" In such cases, an intuitively perfect pirouette is often witnessed, but this technique only works on those riders who have yet to reach menopause. Well, maybe not. In an attempt to achieve the perfect pirouette, some riders watch videotapes of ballerinas performing the movement, envisioning how to translate the dancers' flawless transitions and balance to the dressage arena. Certain top riders have been known to take the analogy one step further and actually wear tutus during their training sessions. One famous rider actually insists that both her horse and her trainer, who happens to be a guy, also wear tutus, but I'm not recommending this because... well, because I just made it up and it's silly.

Piaffe and Passage

The easiest way to perform these excruciatingly difficult movements is to buy a horse that has already been trained to do them. Failing that, you, your trainer and an assistant are going to have to spend a lot of time in the ring with a lunge line and a tapper. It's going to be expensive, but you've already spent a fortune to get your horse to this point anyway, so you may as well pull out the old checkbook again. There are shortcuts, however, that you may want to consider.

Try this: set up a TV and VCR in the stall and play tapes of Ulla Salzgeber, Sue Blinks and the great Klimke performing piaffe and passage as they were meant to be performed. Play the tapes repeatedly throughout the week (I didn't mention that you should make sure that your horse is in the stall at the time—I kind of took it for granted that you would assume that). If your horse doesn't get it, then, as a punishment, play old tapes of Regis and Kathy Lee or Gilligan's Island or perhaps the Gong Show (actually, I liked the Gong Show—I wish they would bring it back).

Apparently, a group of really dedicated rich people have actually created a huge molasses pit in which to perfect their piaffe. So count yourself lucky if you live near any Tar pits, or if you work in a Jello factory. Better still, find a small piece of land that nobody uses, top it with loads of soil and soak it down until it becomes a muddy quagmire. Then try riding your horse through it—voila!— Instant passage! Alternatively, move to Vermont in the spring.

There are famous trainers who prefer to use the volte for teaching piaffe so that the horse is always bent. Personally, I would not recommend this because I have no idea what it means. But, hey, that's just me. Believe it or not, the most effective training method for transitioning from the piaffe to the passage has been in use for centuries, it's the old carrot and stick trick. Just tie a carrot to the end of your whip, perform a piaffe then then dangle the carrot in front of your horse's nose and a seamless transition to passage will follow.

Summary

Well, that just about wraps it up—you are now ready to perform a Grand Prix test. You are among the elite of the sport, the crème de la crème, the top of the milk as the Irish say. But at whatever level you ride, whatever movement you perform, remember that the key to obtaining excellence in dressage is impulsion. Master impulsion, that wonderful thrust from the hind end, and together with good contact, you will have a sound foundation for any movement. Impulsion, contact and, of course, suppleness. With suppleness you can control the impulsion, and achieve perfect straightness. Concentrate on impulsion, contact, suppleness and straightness, not forgetting balance of course. Focus on all of these aspects, impulsion, contact, suppleness, straightness, balance and you will achieve perfect collection. So there you have it, impulsion, contact, suppleness, straightness, balance and collection. Did I mention lightness? Perhaps it's so obvious it goes without saying, lightness plus rhythm. Impulsion, contact, suppleness, straightness, balance, collection, lightness and rhythm are all that you will ever need. And naturally stay relaxed throughout. Impulsion, contact, suppleness, straightness, balance, collection, lightness, rhythm and relaxation are the building blocks of the perfect ride. What could be easier?

Finally, as you progress through the levels you will encounter many difficulties and setbacks but always remember this: the problem is never ever with you, and we all know that it's never with your horse. The problem may be with your trainer or with your saddle or with the ring conditions or with the judges but, more than likely, the problem is with your spouse.

The Gromit Test
How to sneak into heaven through the back door

"A house without a dog is the house of a scoundrel."

Portuguese Proverb

If you are a horse lover, then you are probably also a dog lover. It seems every horse owner also owns at least one dog, having discovered that the joy of an unconditional relationship with both of these wonderful animals, horse and dog, greatly enhances the quality of one's life. But it is not life that is the theme of this piece.... au contraire mon ami, the theme is the afterlife.

So please listen up now, because I'm going to share with you something vitally important regarding your chances of getting into heaven, particularly if you intend to die in the near or distant future. Normally you would not discover this piece of information until you actually die, which is why it is so important, because the only people that know it up until now are....well, are dead.

I found out the secret by accident. You see, I have a Golden Retriever named Gromit, who is not the friendliest dog in the world, but he is bloody close. Other dogs—well, Gromit can take them or leave them—but Gromit loves humans with a frenzy that words are impossible to express. Whenever he meets someone new, he goes bounding up to them, his tail swishing up and down like a fiddler's elbow, his pudgy little ass a-waggling. He greets strangers like he is absolutely delighted to make their acquaintance and, if they would only pet him for a moment, then they would have a bosom buddy for life. Gromit can make you feel that you are a very special person and, even on the darkest day, petting him will make you smile. He is very difficult to resist.

Amazingly, some people do resist him. Some people back away from him or even push him away. One German Shepherd owner, who we sometimes meet on our morning walk, actually raises his foot as Gromit approaches. He hasn't kicked Gromit yet, but I have explained to this gentleman if that ever occurred I could recommend an excellent orthodontist whose services he will require. On any type of rebuff, however, Gromit shows sadness and confusion. He simply cannot understand why some strangers are delighted to meet him and others are not. Frankly, neither can I.

Then the answer came to me one evening via the clarity of a couple of hits of really good single malt Scotch whiskey. Gromit's approach is a test—a test of what type of person you are. And, even more amazingly, if you pass the test and pet him, then you go to Heaven when you die. If you rebuff him, however, then unfortunately you end up in the other place. It's as simple as that—well, almost. You actually get five points, and you need a hundred to get into heaven. It turns out that there is a Gromit dog in every town in America, and across the world, placed here by the Supreme Being with the single function of testing everyone at some point in their lives. Maybe your dog is one of them. It doesn't have to be a Golden Retriever, although many of them are. Just pet twenty test dogs during your life and you slide right through the pearly gates—no questions asked. It turns out that all this religious stuff is just a smokescreen, and a load of hocus pocus (which you suspected was the case anyway, didn't you?).

Recently, Gromit and I were in a pet store, the last place you would expect to find a dog hater, when Gromit applied the test to a well-dressed, upper middle-class lady shopper. She pushed Gromit away with obvious disdain. "Control your dog," she sneered at me. I could have understood this comment if he had been humping her leg or something, but he had just simply asked her to pet him in his cute little way. "I'm very sorry, ma'am," I replied, "but it appears that you have failed the test."

"What test?" she demanded.

"Well the Supreme Being—a female by the way— just used this dog to determine if you are worthy to enter heaven when you kick the bucket. You failed the test miserably. The good news is that, from now on, you don't have to worry about doing good works. They are not going to count for squat. Your fate is now determined, so whoop it up and sin your little heart out. The bad news is that you are going to burn in the fires of hell for all eternity. Have a nice day."

So there you have it friends, forget all those sins, sacraments, commandments, credos, prayers, rites and rituals. You simply need to be a dog lover. As a special bonus, I am also at liberty to reveal that if you are a dog lover and a horse lover, *and* have a weakness for good single malt Scotch then, you will be awarded a really prestigious horse property in suburban heaven. So look for Gromit and I at any dressage show, then come and collect your five points. As for the dog haters, they at least have one consolation—not only are there no dogs in hell, there are no horses either.

UFO Lands on Dressage Ring
Spooks the hell out of everyone

Just remember when you're feeling very down and insecure,
How amazingly unlikely is your birth,
And pray that there's intelligent life somewhere up in space,
Because there's bugger-all down here on earth.

Old Monty Python song

Boarders and staff gasped in disbelief when a Flying Saucer landed in the center of a dressage ring late last Thursday afternoon at Uppersnoot Horse Farm in Wellington, Florida. "It was an unimaginable spectacle," gushed winter boarder, Penelope Martingale. "The thing just suddenly appeared from out of nowhere and hovered over the ring for about a minute before landing. The craft was a silvery cigar-shaped object and stretched from G to D, and from E to B," she continued. "There were three riders in the ring at the time, and I can tell you, you've never seen a horse spook until you've seen him spooked by an alien spacecraft."

A hidden hatch on the side of the craft opened and four aliens emerged, two about ten hands tall and two about six hands. "They all looked like Truman Capote," observed Miguel Sanchez, an employee of the farm, "and they had some type of communication device attached to their mouths that allowed them to converse in American English." The aliens explained that they were a family of four on vacation from the Planet Dorcwad II in the Tetris Nebula, en route to an interstellar family Theme Park in the Crustaceous Constellation. They had landed on earth because their youngsters had to go to the bathroom.

Ms. Suzanne Skippy, proprietor of the farm, and peanut butter heiress, was less than enthusiastic with the entire situation. "This is a prestigious dressage training establishment," she blustered. "How do you think my clientele will feel when they hear that my farm is being used as some kind of cosmic toilet? Why didn't they land in the Ozarks or in New Mexico—the places where they're usually spotted?" Her attitude softened, however, when it was pointed out that an encounter of the third kind such as this would greatly increase the value of her property, plus she would almost certainly be interviewed on the *Today* Show by Matt Lauer. She reluctantly agreed to allow them to use the employees' washroom.

By that time a smallish crowd had gathered around the aliens and gaped at them in awe. Someone asked the adult aliens which one was the male and which the female, as they both looked exactly the same. They replied that they were both females, and that males had become extinct on their planet several millennia ago. They had managed to preserve some male DNA which they used for reproduction, but otherwise the planet was a lot more peaceful and serene without the male gender. Several heads in the crowd nodded approval and someone was heard to mutter "lucky bastards." Then someone asked how they had learned the English language. They explained that they had been monitoring earth's TV and radio transmissions, and they particularly looked forward to each episode of *Friends*. They were curious to know if Rachel had married that dweeb Ross yet.

Then it was the aliens' turn to ask questions of the earthlings. Firstly they asked what was the origin of the letters that marked out the ring that they had landed upon. They wanted to know if they represented some ancient runes, or the initials of famous people, or maybe even something to do with Paul Revere. The earthlings could only mutter, and shuffle their feet. Next the aliens asked about the last presidential election. They said that they were aware that a bloodless coup d'etat had taken place in the United States centered right there in Florida. Knowing what a freedom loving people Americans were they felt sure that the usurpers would have been tossed out by now. Once again, the earthlings muttered and shuffled their feet. The embarrassment was lifted when someone asked the aliens if they would like something to eat. Perhaps they might enjoy a tofu burger or a watercress sandwich on wheat bread. They declined, but they declared that they could murder a quarter-pounder with cheese Happy Meal. Unfortunately, no one present knew what that was, so the visitors had to settle for some baked brie on sesame seed crackers accompanied by a pleasant little bottle of Beaujolais Noveau.

Just about that time a police car arrived, and aliens and earthlings alike were mortified when Officer Jack Grazzino, one of West Palm's finest, issued a citation to the

aliens for operating a vehicle without a valid Florida license. Fortunately, it was quietly pointed out to Officer Jack that this encounter was probably the most important event in recorded history, so he agreed to let the aliens off with just a warning. Officer Jack declared however that INS officers were on their way and might not be as lenient.

So the aliens departed, but not before their youngsters were given a ride around the dressage ring on Daisy, a schooling mare. They took with them parting gifts from their new human friends that included a picture of Sigourney Weaver, several carrots, a salad shooter and a blue ribbon for Training Level, Test 1. The spacecraft then whooshed off into the setting Palm Beach sun. Junior rider Mandi McLeod had taped the entire proceedings on her new VHS camcorder, but unfortunately had forgotten to remove the lens cover. Nevertheless, all who had witnessed the event agreed that, as close encounters go, this had been a proud moment for the sport of dressage.

Snippets of Dressage History # IVIII:
The extended trot of the Light Brigade

"Forward, the Light Brigade!"
Was there a man dismay'd?
Not tho' the soldiers knew
*   Someone had blunder'd:*
Their's not to make reply,
Their's not to reason why,
Their's but to do and die:
Into the valley of Death
*   Rode the six hundred.*

Alfred Lord Tennyson

A little known, and less understood, fact of military history is that the heroic yet suicidal charge of the Light Brigade was actually caused by a dressage horse. This famous cavalry charge occurred in 1853 at the battle of Balaclava during the Crimean War, a conflict that pitted Tsarist Russia against an alliance of Britain, France and Turkey. It was the first time in almost a thousand years that Britain and France had actually been on the same side. This caused a lot of confusion between the British and

French Generals who kept mistakenly ordering their troops to attack each other, to the great amusement of the Russians.

During the battle of Balaclava, some Ruskies snuck up on a group of British artillerymen having their afternoon cup of tea and stole their cannons. A furious Lord Raglan, the British Commander, witnessed this incident. "Go get those bloody cannon," he bellowed at his Light Cavalry commander, Lord Cardigan, who was suffering from a wicked bad hangover. "What bloody cannon?" replied Cardigan testily. "Those bloody cannon over there," Raglan bellowed, pointing furiously into the distance. The commonly held historical belief is that Cardigan mistakenly thought that Raglan pointed not at the stolen British cannon, but at the Russian artillery batteries that lined a long wide valley straight ahead. It came to be known as the Valley of Death.

The truth however, is somewhat different. Lord Cardigan knew exactly which cannon Lord Raglan was referring to. Unfortunately Cardigan was riding a spirited Westphalian mare named Turtle Neck, and when he gave his mare the signal to advance, she mistook it for an aid to perform an extended trot across the diagonal. This took rider and horse directly toward the Valley of Death and before Cardigan could make a correction the entire Light Brigade, five regiments of the finest British cavalry had followed them. His Lordship, not wanting his men to think that he was lacking in the basics of dressage horsepersonship, continued with the error until it was too late to turn back.

In horror the British and French General Staff watched from the heights overlooking the valley as these brave but poorly led troopers, Hussars, Light Dragons and

Lancers, in their magnificently accoutered uniforms, mounted on beautiful, shining steeds trotted forward in perfect lines to their doom. All who took part knew it was suicide, yet none reined in. "C'est magnifique," exclaimed the French Commander, "mais c'est ne pas la guerre," which translated means, "excellent conformation, but the impulsion of the third rank lacks tenacity."

Cannons to the right of them,
Cannons to the left...
Volley'd and thunder'd;...
Into the jaws of Death,...
Rode the six hundred.

Despite the slaughter of man and horse, the Light Brigade pressed home their desperate charge and reached the Russian guns at the end of the valley, sabers slashing and lances thrusting at their tormentors. Then those few who could still ride or walk straggled back the way they had come. Lord Cardigan and Turtleneck survived the charge, which is more than can be said for most of his men and their mounts. The Russian General at C gave the 7th Hussars a 71%, as did the British judge at M, but the French Judge at B marked everyone low, out of Gallic envy. Overall however the 7th Hussars were awarded the blue ribbon, posthumously of course. Lord Cardigan was heard to remark to the few survivors after they returned from the famous charge, "I hope that you see this whole thing as a learning experience. You can now understand the trouble that can ensue from putting on too much lower leg."

I Married a Dressage Show Secretary
And lived to tell the tale

Every year, during the first week of May, all hell breaks loose in our house. My normally laid-back and stress-free existence is shattered by the advent of the New England Dressage Association Spring Show, for which my wife volunteers as Secretary.

In this vital capacity, she receives all of the applications, schedules the classes and the rides, creates and prints the programs, schedules the judges, deposits the checks, and fields an awful lot of phone calls. Of course I help her—that's my job. Our family room, which I keep spotlessly clean and neat because that's also my job, is suddenly transformed into mayhem central. Boxes of applications appear labeled "Complete," "Incomplete," "Undecipherable." Three ring binders containing unknown but vital information abound; computer software and manila folders are scattered everywhere. A huge printer is brought in from somewhere, and a special secretary's desk appears from our storage room, (a piece of furniture that frankly greatly diminishes the early garage sale décor of the living room).

Printers clatter, software pings, telephones ring, papers rustle, Gromit barks, Brian curses. UPS and FedEx delivery people line up at our door to deliver urgently important applications. In short, our boring yet normally tranquil home becomes a zoo. (Metaphorically, of course—it doesn't actually become a zoo. We don't invite the horses in for cocktails or anything. We tried that once, just to see how they would behave in a domestic setting, but it was a disaster. Gus took up the whole couch, guzzling an entire bottle of Tanqueray gin in one gulp, and we couldn't get the channel remote away from Marty. "Back to the barn for both of you, my lads," said I).

Where was I? Oh yes, the ringing phone. Now my wife works during the day, God love her, so I'm the one that takes most of the phone calls. In fact, for the last two years she has been away on business trips for the crucial week when the contestants receive the ride times that she sends them. Have you ever noticed that the ride times in any show that you have entered are always bad times? Have you ever said, "Wow, look at these times, they are just *perfect?*" Be honest, now.

Where was I? Oh yes, the ringing phone. My wife's instructions to me are simple: be courteous, take a message, and tell the caller that she will return their call later in the evening. Being courteous is the easy part—after all I am British—but just simply taking a message is much more difficult for me to comply with. As a "house husband" and "horse minder," I don't get the opportunity to talk to many people anymore as I did when I had a real job, so any type of social interaction is something I crave. When telemarketers call I usually buy what they are selling, just to

keep them on the line so I have someone to talk with. (I've changed long distance carrier three times). Frankly, it's not a situation that they are used to, to say the least. After a few minutes, they start to get uncomfortable and look for excuses to get rid of me. It's a wonderful role reversal that I cherish.

Where was I? Oh yes, the ringing phone. So suddenly, with all of these intriguing dressage people calling, I'm just expected to simply take a message? I do try, but I generally fail miserably and grab at the chance of chatting away. Usually the conversations are interesting and cordial, but occasionally I can't help being the smart-ass that I'm genetically programmed to be. Here are a few examples:

Driiiing - Driiing

Yes, hello, this is Jocelyn Jones. I'm entered for the NEDA spring show, but I'm afraid that I'm going to have to scratch.

Well Jocelyn, I'm sorry to hear that. But my advice is don't scratch, because you are only going to make it worse. You should put some ointment on it, and call me in the morning.

Driiing - Driiing

Hello. Is this NEDA? This is L.J. Caversson. I received your postcard with my times for the spring show, but it indicates that I'm entered into Second Level Test 2 Open, whereas I wanted Second Level Test 2 Qualifying, or Third Level Test 1 Adult Amateur, Non-Qualifying. Failing that I would take Third Level Test 2, Qualifying or Open.

I'm sorry, L.J., my wife will have to call you back later, because, in all openness, I not qualified to help you.

Driing - Driiing

Yes, hello, my name is Debbie and I want to enter the spring show, but the entry form says that I need to have a parent sign the form if I am younger than twenty-one. I'm only nineteen and my parents and I are estranged. What should I do?

Well, Debbie, my advice is to lie about your age. Who's going to know? That's what I did when I was a teenager. Better still, just forge your mother's signature on the form, which, incidentally, will be good practice if you ever get hold of her checkbook or credit cards.

Driiing - Driiing

Hello my name is Nancy. I'm calling about the Dressage Show. Who is this?

Hello Nancy, this is Brian. Maybe I can help you or, if not, I can take a message.

Oh Brian, I'm sure that you are very busy, and it's so nice of you to give up your time. I have a teensy, weensy favor to ask that really is not that important, so it's okay if you say no.

Well, we try and accommodate any reasonable request. What do you need?

What I need is…you know you have such a charming accent. I just love a man with an accent. Where are you from?

I'm from England, originally.

Oh, that's wonderful—which part?

All of me.

Oh you English! Always joking. I just love your sense of humor. And the English are always such charming people. Gallant and charming.

Ah Nancy, I think it's you that has all the charm. You're trying to schmooze something out of me, now aren't you? And do you know what?—It's going to work. You are so delightful that whatever you want, I'm going to get it for you.

Oh Brian, you are so special! I need my second ride time changed from 9.10 a.m. to about 11 a.m. Can you do that for me?

Nancy, consider it done. My wife is as susceptible to charm as I am.

Driiing - Driiing

Yes, this is Andrea Morningbrook-Smythe. Are you one of these NEDA people? Look, I've booked a stall for your show, and I want it to be close to my friends. I also want the stall to be situated at the end of the row, to the front, and

I don't want to be in a row with any stallions, mares or Arabians. Is that clear?

Yes, Alice, that's very clear. I'll pass that requirement onto my wife.

Andrea, it's Andrea.

What?

You called me Alice. My name is Andrea.

I'm sorry about that, but not to worry. I will not forget to make sure that my wife gets this message. Thank you for calling, Allison, bye now.

Driing - Driing

Yes, this is Leona Leadbottom. I've just received a card from you today that states that I am wait-listed for the NEDA show, and my number on the wait list is 30. I'm assuming this is a mistake.

Well, Leona, which part do you think is a mistake? Is it that you received a card, or that you are wait-listed, or that you are number 30?

Well, I certainly didn't expect to be wait-listed—I am riding Prix St. Georges and Intermediare 1, you know.

I'm sorry, but the show filled up quickly. It's first come, first served.

Of course, but I'm sure that you give those riding the higher levels preference over the lower levels.

No, we don't. If all the entries that fill up all of the rides are Training Level, then we will have a Training level show.

That's preposterous! Your show will have no status without the higher levels competing.

I doubt it, Leona. Those riding the higher levels are

experienced enough to know that they have to get their entries in early for the popular shows. The rules are the same across the nation, as any volunteer will tell you. By the way, have you ever considered volunteering to help at a show? It is very rewarding.

Driiing- Driiing

Hello, this is Emily Entwhistle. I received a postcard from you stating that the paperwork that I sent in to ride a USAeq Qualifying Freestyle is incomplete. Can you please tell me what I need?

Well, Emily, all that we received from you is a show entry form. The additional paperwork for a USAeq Qualifying Freestyle is spelled out in your Omnibus, but it's quite simple. First, you will need to have an AHSA membership number—I mean an USAeq number of course, but everyone still calls it ASHA. You will need to send a copy of the ASHA membership verification for the rider, the owner, the trainer, the horse and the coach. If any of these are not members, then you need to send an additional $15 per membership fee plus $5 each for the dressage discipline. Unless you are a junior rider, in which case there is no dressage fee. If you need a score to receive an end-of-year USDF award, then you will need to send proof of USDF membership for the rider, the owner, the trainer and the horse. Finally, you will have to have ridden the highest test of the level of your freestyle and have scored over 60% at a competition prior to this one. That's about it, Emily. Nothing too complex. Oh, and don't forget your Coggins and, of course, your payment. Emily? Emily? Emily, are you still there?

Know Your Horse's Anatomy
A primer for dressage husbands on horse guts

Nothing gives me greater pleasure than helping my brother dressage husbands in our eternal quest to support our wives by understanding the intricacies of the sport they so dearly love. Actually, that's a big fat lie. There are a heck of a lot more things that give me greater pleasure. A bag of Doritos gives me greater pleasure. But I have a duty to perform, so here once again is Mr. Dressage Husband with a bucketful of knowledge to help you, the novice husband, to converse with your wife and her equestrian friends in a semi-intelligent fashion. This time the subject is 'Horse guts—inside and out.'

Most dressage husbands know which end the oats go in and which end the oats come out, but that's usually about the extent of their knowledge of horse anatomy. Still, we are well aware that these horse people have a language all their own when it comes to describing parts of the animal. Whenever dressage people talk about their horses, they may as well be speaking in Cantonese as far as an outsider is concerned. Often they will use a special horse malady as an excuse for why they performed so badly during a test. They'll say something like, "We would have scored a 72 if he hadn't developed a palpitating pastern going in, instead of the 45 that we actually scored." So here then is an attempt to lift the mask of obscurity from some of these cryptically named horse parts.

Like most critters, a horse consists of a bunch of bones joined together to form a skeleton, held in place by muscles, tendons, ligaments and other bits. Inside the skeleton is where you'll find all the vital organs crammed together, marinating in blood. The whole mess is wrapped in skin to prevent any parts from falling out, and the skin is covered in hair that they once used to stuff into couches. Okay, that's enough of the technical terms. It's best if we don't concentrate too long on the internal organs because, frankly, the insides of a horse are really disgusting. On the outside, a horse may be a thing of beauty, sleek, strong, with magnificent shining muscles. On the inside, it's gross. All of the internal organs are much larger than most other animals. For example, the kidneys are the size of watermelons and the intestines would stretch from Montreal to Quebec, including losing their way twice because they couldn't understand the French road signs.

First, let's examine the **bones**. For centuries there has existed some unnatural, unspoken financial arrangement between domestic animals and veterinarians, whereby, if an animal can find a way to hurt itself, it will. Horses are the worst perpetrators of this macabre alliance. If there exists the smallest protuberance in it's stall or paddock, a horse will cut itself open; if there is the smallest pebble in the paddock a horse will break a bone. Horse bones break like they were made of balsa wood, although they appear to be extremely strong. Remember Samson slew the Philistines with the jawbone of an ass, or maybe it was the ass bone of a giraffe—I forget. One horse bone is united with another horse bone using duct tape—no, just kidding, using cartilage, to form a joint (in the sixties we made joints out of some of the weirdest stuff, but never cartilage). Veterinarians use the word articulation as a synonym for joint, and how bones are joined together is best captured by the old song:

Dem Bones, Dem Bones, Dem Horse Bones,
Oh, the **scapula** *bone's articulated to the* **hock** *bone,*
The **hock** *bone's articulated to the* **sesamoid** *bone,*
The **sesamoid** *bone's articulated to the* **cannon** *bone,*
The **cannon** *bone's articulated to the* **navicular** *bone,*
Hear the name of the Lord, etc.etc.

Other parts of the horse's body that are important include the **croup**, which is situated on the upper part of the body between the loins and the tail. The **croup** extends down on each side from a line drawn from the lower edge of the point of the hip to the point of the buttock. So what *is* the point of the buttock? I mean, horses don't sit down, so why do they need buttocks? I suppose it's kind of like that *Why did Adam need a navel?* thing.

The **fetlock** is that piece of the mane that hangs down over the horse's face—no, wait, that's the **forelock**. The **fetlock** is another hank of hair that sticks out somewhere, I'm just not sure where. The **brisket** is part of the lower chest, which can become enlarged if the horse eats too much cabbage, carrots and potatoes. The **withers** is a bony ridge on the back of the horse, but nobody really knows the exact location. The **shank** is part of the lower leg below the knee. The word is derived from American football, when the punter mistakenly hits the ball with his leg rather than his foot and shanks the ball into the bleachers for a five-yard loss. The **dock** is the upper part of the tail. The late, great singer Otis Redding was a famous horse lover, but his dressage abilities were woefully lacking because he insisted on riding too far back in the saddle. As he passed, other riders would snicker, "There goes old Otis again—Sitting on the Dock of the Bay." (Okay, I know that was bad. But you try making this stuff funny!)

An important part of the horse is the hoof—all four of them, actually. The **hoof** is divided into the **toe**, the **crust**, the **wall**, the **frog**, the **cleft of the frog** and the **eye of a newt**. On the lower part of the leg is located the **hock**, which to other horses is the most sensuous part of the body. "Wow man, check out the **hocks** on that filly over there," one gelding will often say to another. Although, of course, being geldings, checking out hocks is just an exercise in frustration. The **gaskin** is made of a hard rubbery substance and is situated between the **thigh** and the **hock** to prevent oil from leaking out. You can locate it by a line drawn forward from the point of the **hock**. Of course, I'm referring here to imaginary lines. I'm not suggesting that you grab a magic marker and draw lines all over your horse, although that might be fun if you own a grey. Speaking of magic markers, I wonder if Appaloosa owners ever have an urge to connect the dots?

The **pastern** is two columns of bones located just above the hoof, and is sponsored by a company that makes really good Italian food. The **chestnuts** are those horny growths just above the knees, which many people believe are where the foal's legs were joined together in the womb, but are, in fact, just a bad case of eczema. The **nervous systems** in a dressage horse is plural because every system in his entire being is nervous. Dressage horses will generally spook at anything. They will even spook at things that don't exist, on the conviction that something is going to be worth spooking at in that place, sometime in the future. Horses also have **fore-arms** and **elbows** although, you may have noticed, they don't have arms. I guess they must have run out of words.

So there you have it, my brothers—all the common words worth knowing about a horse's body. For the much more technical terms of a horse's anatomy, please refer to the attached diagram.

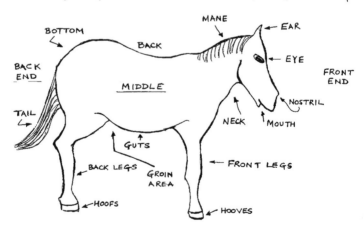

KNOW YOUR HORSE — TECHNICAL TERMS FOR YOUR HORSE'S BODY

(NOTE: BACK LEGS HAVE HOOFS, FRONT LEGS HAVE HOOVES, GO FIGURE)

Illustration courtesy of the author

Snippets of Dressage History # L:
François Baucher makes up his mind

 S till considered crazy after all these years, Frenchman François Baucher (1793—1873), was one of the most controversial of the great dressage masters of yore. He is chiefly remembered as one of the early proponents of the *round-and-deep* method of riding that is finding such popularity today among the top riders. Monsieur Baucher (pronounced *Baucher*) was also unique in that he devised two very different methods of training during his life.

Baucher called his first method *Effet d'Ensemble* (literally: British Parliament) which he developed while working in the circus, where he doubled as both the horse trainer and the last clown to get out of the little red car. In the Effet d'Ensemble method, Baucher sought to overcome resistance by altering the center of gravity of the horse. To this end, he enlisted the help of two famous scientists, G.S. Ohm for the resistance part and Sir Isaac Newton for the gravity part, but they both lost interest when they began squabbling over whose law was more important.

Baucher remained undaunted. He was convinced that his method would revolutionize horsepersonship and he claimed that he could transform an untrained horse into Grand Prix quality in, like, an afternoon. The *Effet d'Ensemble* method, in addition to the whole center of gravity thing, relies on using the legs as the primary aid and, in essence, disconnects the movement of the front end and the hind end from the topline. It might not be evident to you exactly what that means. In truth it is probably too complex for most riders to understand—I understand it, of course—but I simply do not have the time or the patience to explain it to you right now.

The Baucher method had many detractors, but they could not argue with his results. He demonstrated the efficacy of his method by training horses to canter backward, pirouette backward and canter backward on three legs (really)! The other great dressage masters of the day, mostly German, were not impressed. "Big deal!" they cried (in German) "So you can canter backward, but why would you *want* to?" While Baucher sold his training method to the French cavalry, the German cavalry relied on the classical high school methods (so called because the movements were so easy any high school kid could do them). The final clash of the methods occurred at the battle of Sedan in 1870 during the Franco-Prussian war. Whereas the German cavalry performed with their usual discipline, the normally formidable French cavalry were at sixes and sevens all over the battlefield, charging forward, backward, sideways— some even charging backward into their own infantry. Consequently the French lost the battle and the war. When the French generals finally collared Monsieur Baucher, "It's

back to the circus for you, my lad," they cried, dragging him away.

Now in disgrace, Baucher tried to expand his method into even more radical movements. He experiment-ed with the horse going forward but now the rider going backwards, a movement he quickly abandoned due to the excessive number of rider injuries that occurred during equestrian collisions. Then one day, while performing in the circus, a heavy chandelier fell on him (really). As he lay there in the sawdust, elephant droppings all around, he experi-enced an epiphany. "Sacré bleu!" he exclaimed (transla-tion—bloody hell!). "Riding backwards? What was I think-ing?" It was soon after that Francois Baucher developed his second method.

Because the accident had damaged his legs, Baucher now sought the balance he desired by using hardly any aids at all. He called it the *main sans jambes, jambes sans main* method (translation: look ma, no hands! look ma, no legs!). It also became known as *Equitation in your*

Jammies, and appeared to be in direct opposition to his first method, allowing the horse almost total freedom in its forward momentum. This second method was a lot more boring than the first method, but yet more difficult to comprehend. So if you thought that I was having trouble explaining the first method, then you can bet your saddle that there is no way I'm going to even attempt to BS my way through the second method. Suffice it to say that old Francois was accepted back into the dressage fold, even by the classical dressage masters, who believed that Baucher had finally seen the light. Actually he probably didn't see the light, otherwise he would have jumped out of the way before it hit him.

Today there are several aspects of dressage that bear Baucher's influence. For example, his first method is clearly a forerunner of the modern "round and deep" riding technique. He was the first to perform a lengthy sequence of one-tempi changes, which he perfected on a trip to Arizona. We have a Baucher bit in our barn somewhere, although I couldn't tell you what it looks like, and I believe that almost every racehorse that I ever bet on was trained in Baucher's cantering backward method. So there you have it, another provocative glimpse into the fascinating and colorful, yet never sordid, world of the discipline of dressage equitation.

Dressage Mafia Strike Again
Sinister goings-on from dressage hooligans

The Executive Board of the United States Dressage Federation met in emergency session last Thursday to address what it called 'the unacceptable growth of criminal activity' in the United States dressage community. Denying the existence of what some have termed, "The Dressage Mafia," the board nevertheless conceded that certain "unsavory elements" have infiltrated the normally law abiding, upper middle class dressage environment. Regardless of how the USDF tries to downplay the problem, the concern that dressage needs to clean house arose after a series of recent startling revelations of criminal activity that have shocked the U.S. dressage world.

The latest exposé occurred last week when it was revealed that certain 'shifty-looking characters' had attended some of the more important dressage competitions on the east coast and had 'opened book.' A horse trailer was being used as a betting window where substantial betting activity was taking place on CDI competitions.

Apparently, "point spread" betting was also in effect based on freestyle scores.

Special Agent Wayne C. Hobble of the FBI, Equine Division, has been assigned to the case and told reporters last evening that the FBI were closing in on the perpetrators. "The suspect horse trailer has been spotted at Dressage at Devon, the Heidelburg Cup and at the Gladstone U.S. Selection Trials," he stated. "It won't be long before arrests are made. Frankly, the whole thing makes me sick to my stomach," he continued. "Not only have these people besmirched the purity of the sport of dressage by their gambling racket but now we have reports of them threatening the judges." A German judge was apparently accosted at Devon by a scruffy looking individual wearing an old Eddie Bauer anorak, who suggested that the judge should mark certain riders low on their canter pirouettes, if he ever wanted to see the fatherland again with teeth in his head.

Agent Hobble added that the gang's criminal activities have expanded to coercing protection money from dressage show vendors. And, for the first time, it appears they followed through on their threats of violence when the guy who sells those little therapeutic magnets refused to pay them. "It was an ugly sight—a very ugly sight," Agent Hobble recounted. "They made him swallow all of his magnets, then hung him up on his own refrigerator. The poor man is still in hospital, suffering from a bad case of freezer burn."

"We are fairly certain," continued Hobble, "that the gang consists of a group of renegade dressage husbands who have reached the end of their tether, so to speak. Their ringleader is apparently an older man, somewhat charming and debonair, who is always seen in the company of a friendly Golden Retriever. He has a definite foreign accent, the man not the Golden Retriever, that is neither Italian nor Russian. According to eyewitnesses, he sports a certain Anglo-Irish twang—sort of similar to the Beatles. If you spot him at a dressage show, call the police but do not approach him—he is extremely dangerous and is believed to be armed with a sharp hoof pick."

The activities of this criminal element were first reported at dressage shows last season when they began to charge people 50 cents to use the porta-potties. The scam was successful because people are not going to argue over 50 cents when they have to go, and afterwards are generally relieved enough to believe it was worth the money.

Flushed by this success (hah!), the gang then moved on to more serious crimes. The first report came from Teresa Carbuncle, owner of Tumbleweed Farm in Austin, Texas. Explained Ms. Carbuncle, "I was approached by two pallid-looking men who demanded that I rent them space in the hayloft of my barn. Naturally I refused, but when they

threatened to squirt wormer paste into my new show boots, I had no choice but to comply. Imagine my horror when, two days later, I went up to my hayloft and found it stuffed with illegal dressage merchandise." Using Ms. Carbuncle's hayloft as a distribution point, the gang traveled around all the prestigious dressage farms in the Southwest, peddling the merchandise from the back of a trailer, claiming it was brand name, top-of-the-line dressage equipment. All the items, however, are clever forgeries manufactured, it is believed, in Mozambique. At first glance, they look genuine enough, but a close examination of the brands' labels will reveal that the names are slightly different then those that they are supposed to represent. For example, Schumacher bridles are in fact spelt Shoemaker, and Hermes saddles are spelt Herpes saddles—a name that you may not want to brag about to your friends. Dehner boots are spelt Daimler boots. Daimler is not known for boots; they manufacturer automobiles—high quality automobiles to be sure, but automobiles nonetheless. A close look at the label for a Pikeur shadbelly will show it to be spelt Pricker shagbelly, which is, in fact, believed to be a position in the Karma Sutra.

Although the FBI claim to be close to making arrests, they clearly missed their opportunity at the Green Mountain Horse Association dressage show last July in Woodstock, Vermont. The dressage gang was there in force, terrorizing the local populace, by getting drunk on hard lemonade and then drag racing their horse trailers through the center of the quaint little town. State and local police, plus the FBI, closed in but the gang scattered into the many winding back roads of the area. They did manage to isolate the ringleader, however, in his 20-year-old, two-horse gooseneck, and chased him onto Highway 91 north. In a scene reminiscent of a reality TV cop show, police cars pursued the trailer along the highway, while helicopters tracked it overhead, as it raced towards the Canadian border at breakneck speeds approaching close to 45 mph. Just five miles from the border, the trailer blew a tire, spun around and came to an abrupt halt. With weapons drawn, the police closed in but suddenly the trailer's rear doors burst open and out sprang the suspect mounted on a beautiful ebony warmblood. The police were so taken by surprise that the horse and rider cantered off, escaping into the thick woods. Sighed Agent Hobble, "So where are the Royal Canadian Mounted Police when you need them?"

"Make no mistake," concluded Agent Hobble, "Sooner or later we are going to round up this gang of villains, and put them on probation for a very long time. If it was my decision, I would horsewhip them first, but that's probably what turned them bad in the first place."

This Just In: Tidbits of Dressage News
United States Rider stiffed at World Cup

The United States dressage community was justifiably proud of the American dressage team in capturing the silver medal at the recent World Equestrian Games. The event this year was held in Spain, (an interesting choice given that the Spanish national sport is bull fighting, the ritualistic torture and slaughter of beautiful, majestic animals). Unfortunately the euphoria of the American team on their accomplishment was sullied by the fact that team member Dottie McDougal rode a near perfect ride in the Freestyle portion of the competition, but was placed only fourth. Clearly the best ride of the day, only the British judge awarded her first place. If Dottie had have been awarded first place by all the judges in the freestyle, as she deserved, she would have won the bronze medal in the overall individual competition and would be the first American to ever win an individual medal at the Dressage World Cup.

The placing was even more difficult to understand given that the third place finisher in the Freestyle was German rider Gertrude Wiener, who actually scratched before the test. The German judge, Viktor Von Dusseldork, when finally cornered, was asked why Gertrude was awarded the bronze medal when she didn't actually compete. He replied that he was well aware that Gertrude didn't ride, but he felt justified in awarding her high marks because he had seen her ride that test in other competitions, and was sure that, had she actually competed, she would have performed splendidly.

Olympic Dressage Site used to be Brothel

As reported recently in *Dressage Today*, workman in Athens excavating an area to construct a Dressage Arena for the upcoming 2004 Olympic Games, uncovered a site of an ancient Greek brothel. Honestly, this is true—even I couldn't make something up as bizarre as that. Of course, the first question that comes to mind is: how did they know it was a brothel? I mean, we are talking underground ruins from 2,500 years ago. What distinguishing features did this ancient ruin have that made archeologists say to the workmen, "Dig no more here, Zorba and Dimitri, looks like you've unearthed an ancient house of ill repute." One could understand it if they had dug up, say, a bowling alley or even a pizza parlor. Maybe the ruins comprised of a lot of little rooms, but then they could have easily once been a prison or even a guesthouse. Perhaps there were some really racy mosaics on the floor, or ancient graffiti scrawled on the walls like, "Socrates was here and had a fine time, but Plato of course never showed up." The second question that comes to mind is, "Being Greek, what type of brothel was it?" But we are not going to pursue that question any further.

A better explanation is that those archaeologists had no idea what type of building the ruins once where. More than likely, some FEI dressage honchos, knowing that excavations anywhere in Athens is bound to unearth ancient ruins, slipped the archaeologists a bundle of drachmas to pronounce the ruins a brothel, in the hope of attracting more spectators to the dressage events.

Judge Awards Points for Shiny Boots

Last Thursday, a judge at a dressage show in New York reportedly awarded a competitor two extra points for the shine on her boots. The competitor, Julie Alnwick, riding her lovely Dutch Warmblood, Jason, in a Fourth Level class was astounded to find the extra two points added to her final score, with the judge's notation saying, "nice ride; here is a couple of points for your shiny boots." This is believed to be the first time that a dressage judge has added extra points for appearance. Commented Julie, "I'm delighted that a judge has recognized the time and effort that I spent in trying to look my best. I was up at 4 a.m. and at the show grounds by 4.30. By the time I braided Jason, cleaned the stall, fed him breakfast, groomed him, then grabbed a bite to eat myself, I only had a half hour to prepare myself before my ride at 8 a.m. I spent fifteen minutes polishing my boots until you needed dark glasses to look at them."

The judge in question, Mrs. Margaret Thadcastle, who wishes to remain anonymous, was heard to remark, "I just thought that it was time that we judges made the competitors aware that we appreciate the lengths they must go to in order to prepare their ensemble before each test." Needless to say, show vendors sold out of boot polish very soon after.

Progress Reported on Equine Genetic Engineering

A spokesperson for Equigen, a California based company on the bleeding edge of equine genetic alterations, recently announced that they had made some interesting progress in their quest to produce the 'perfect' dressage horse.

According to spokesperson Dr. Daisy McPherson, Equigen research scientists have managed to isolate the equine gene that causes a horse to come off the bit. Apparently this is a major step towards their goal of producing a perfectly balanced, obedient and highly intelligent dressage horse. A month ago, the company announced that it had genetically altered a horse that was so smart that he would open the gate of his paddock, walk over to the manure pile, do his business on the pile, then walk back to his paddock, locking the gate behind him. Naturally the equestrian world was skeptical, particularly in light of Equigen's past controversial failures in their attempt to clone a Grand Prix dressage horse.

The company abandoned its cloning experiments last August after it failed not only to produce a quality dressage horse, but also failed to clone a quality rider. Their attempts to clone a perceptive judge also proved a disaster, as were their efforts to clone a bevy of appreciative spectators. Further, Equigen was severely criticized for selling off its herd of failed cloned horses without informing the buyers of the source of these horses. If your horse whinnies a lot, tends to bite, chews on its stall and is difficult to train, you probably own one of Equigen's failed equine experiments.

Network Television decides not to cover Dressage in Olympics

A spokesperson for NBC Sports announced today that they had reversed their decision to provide full television coverage for the dressage events at the upcoming Olympic games in Athens, Greece. Originally, the network had agreed to feature dressage as the "Sport of the Future" and devote two prime-time hours every evening to televise all rides in Grand Prix, Freestyle and Grand Prix Special classes. It is believed that this would have been the first time that any network, since the invention of the cathode ray tube, has televised dressage. NBC Sports intended to hire John Madden and Dick Albert as the chief commentators and to feature overhead cams, slow motion replays and special cameras attached to competitors' dressage hats. Further, the network intended to have Katie Couric conduct heart-rending interviews with close relatives and pets of competitors who have recently undergone life-threatening surgery, or at least haven't been feeling very well. But now NBC Sports have decided to shelf that plan and revert to the normal network policy of not even mentioning the sport of dressage, let alone televising it.

A spokesperson for the network told reporters that they had conducted a survey of several thousand sports fans and not one had ever heard of dressage, except for one Palm Beach resident who had threatened to call the police if the surveyors bothered her again. Instead of dressage, NBC Sports now intends to cover the increasingly popular new sports of Nude Beach Volleyball and Synchronized Underwater Arm Wrestling.

Snippets of Dressage History # MMIV:
A dressage competition during the Trojan War

A burning, racking controversy has raged for many years among us professional Dressage Historians regarding the exact origin of the sport. Who developed dressage, and when? And why? And what drugs were they taking? And why didn't they just take their money and drop it into the nearest volcano to placate the gods? And who cares? We professional Dressage Historians care, that's who, racked as we are with burning controversy.

Some say the Italians developed dressage in the sixteenth century AD, somewhere between the time the ceiling of the Sistine Chapel was painted and the time the walls of the Vatican staff cafeteria were wallpapered. Other, more objective, experts maintain that dressage actually began in England at the time of Lady Godiva, (see *Snippet Number XXIX: Lady Godiva Reveals All*). Well, it turns out that both of these theories are just a load of old codswallop, due to a recent startling discovery. While excavating an area of Athens to build an equestrian center for the 2004

Olympic games, workmen unearthed ancient scrolls that clearly document the fact that dressage began much further back in history than anyone heretofore or thereafter or even henceforth could possibly have imagined. Apparently dressage goes way back to, like, 1200 years BC—to the time of the legendary Trojan War.

The Trojan War was an epic struggle between the ancient mainland Greeks and one of their colonies on the other side of the Aegean Sea, the city of Troy, located in what is modern day upstate New York. Or maybe it was in modern day Turkey. Anyway, the whole brouhaha started when Paris, the son of the King of Troy, so named because he was always looking for a bit of 'ooh-la-la,' took a fancy to a nubile little Greek number named Helen. So he whisked her away to Troy, to have his wicked way with her. Unfortunately, young Paris was unaware that Helen was the wife of Menelaus, King of Sparta, brother of the mighty Greek overlord Agamemnon. These two royal dudes were real badasses, who make Tony Soprano and his buddies look like Carmelite nuns. The Greeks were always looking for a reason for a good punch-up, even more than we are today, so they declared war on the Trojans and launched a thousand ships to save Helen's honor. After they launched the ships, they realized that perhaps they should have been in them, and so they had to spend the first couple of years of the war building another thousand ships, thereby losing the element of surprise. In the meantime, Helen had married Paris, settled down, had four little Trojans and was moderately happy. Still, there was a score to be settled, so the Greeks invaded in their new ships and besieged the city of Troy for ten years, which is still a record.

At this point, you are probably thinking, "This certainly is a bucketful of mesmerizing history, but when are we going to get to the dressage part which, after all is the subject of this article, not to mention this whole darn book?" Well, hold your horses there, Nellie (hah!). Before we get to dressage there is a little more you should know about the ancient Greeks, who are the most fascinating people yet to inhabit this planet, with the possible exception of the Radio City Music Hall Rockettes. It is important to us Dressage Historians that you are not confused as to the actual ancient Greeks of which we speak. The ancient Greeks in question are not the same ancient Greeks who invented Western civilization, including democracy, theater, medicine, mathematics, all of the sciences, the remote control and barbecue chicken wings. Those particular ancient Greeks, who included such heavy hitters as Aristotle, Socrates, Plato, Pythagorus, Herodotus, Hypocrates, Meningitis and so on, lived during the Golden Age of Ancient Greece. Our ancient Greeks, the ancient Greeks of the Trojan War, were about 700 years more ancient than those dudes, and lived in the Clueless Age of Ancient Greece. They were so ancient that many of them were demi-gods, which means that they were lucky enough to be half-mortal, half-god, due to the fact that their mother, or occasionally their father, was seduced by a god or goddess.

Both of the opposing armies included a fair number of demi-gods and heroes. Theirs were names of great legends, such as Achilles, Ajax and Odysseus for the Greeks, Hector and Aeneas for the Trojans. Both sides were aided and abetted by the gods themselves, who were always up for a bit of mischief. The Greek gods were a wonderfully interesting set of paranoiac characters: one minute they were benevolent, loving and merciful, the next they were petty, jealous and vindictive. And they were always horny, hence the number of demi-gods that abounded. (You rarely hear of demi-gods these days, except for perhaps Reiner Klimke or Anky von Grunsven). With both sides being even, the war dragged on despite great collective and individual battles outside the walls of Troy. By the tenth year, the Greeks had understandably had enough, seeing as they had only brought enough sandwiches to last for a weekend. The Trojans, too, had reached the end of their tether, the war having destroyed their economy, which was based on the manufacture of prophylactics. So the two sides decided to settle the entire war with a single dressage competition.

At the start of the war, neither side rode horses because nobody had figured out how to ride. Instead, they used horses to pull chariots, with a driver and a warrior in each. It was Achilles who finally got tired of this arrangement, standing in a chariot all day, because he suffered from acute tendinitis. "If we could ride on the back of the beasts, then we wouldn't need the damn chariot, and I could save all that money on Bengay," he thought. Then the Goddess Athena appeared to him in a dream and revealed that the reason no one had managed to ride a horse was that they had all tried to mount on the wrong side, the horse's right side. "That's why it's called the 'off' side, because the horse will always throw you off," she explained. The next day Achilles mounted a horse on the left side and from that day forth 'The Age of the Chariot' was over.

As riding horses became popular between the combatants, it quickly became a matter of pride as to who was the better rider. So, it was no surprise when both sides agreed that a horsepersonship competition should decide the winner of the long conflict. It wasn't called 'dressage' yet, because at that time the French had not been invented, nor was it pretty to watch because the saddle, stirrups and bridle were not even on the drawing board. Riders were lucky to score 25%.

Achilles was the Greek champion for the big event, riding the legendary wild horse Arion, who was endowed with the power of speech. The Trojans chose Hector as their champion, riding the winged horse Pegasus. The ring was marked out by gods standing alongside each other forming a rectangle. Down one side stood **H**era the wife of Zeus, then next to her was **S**elene the moon goddess, then **E**ros god of love, then Aphrodite the goddess of love whom the Romans called **V**enus, then **K**ratos the Titan. Along the other side stood **M**edusa, **R**hea, **B**acchus, **P**ollux and one of the **F**uries. At one end was **A**thena herself and at the other stood **C**yclops, keeping an eye on the whole procedure. Now, I'm not suggesting for one minute that is how the dressage letters originated, but you have to agree that it is one hell of a coincidence. Several centaurs acted as judges, naturally.

Achilles rode first. It was a disappointing ride, quite frankly, because Achilles' aids were not well understood by his horse. Arion, the original talking horse, was used to the rider speaking the commands, which, of course is not allowed in dressage. Finally Arion stopped in mid-pirouette and yelled angrily at Achilles to stop digging his heels into his side (in Greek of course). "I don't know what movement you want me to perform, buddy," Arion shouted, "but it's all

Greek to me." This embarrassment caused Achilles to skulk out of the ring. In stark contrast, Hector's ride on Pegasus was magnificent: the extensions were beautiful, the passage a sight to behold, and you've never seen flying changes until you've seen them performed by a horse with wings. The Trojans scored 96.8%, while the Greeks received just 13.5%, and only got that because Achilles didn't fall off.

"Still, let's look on the bright side," Achilles told his compatriots. "At least we got the red ribbon."

Having admitted defeat, the Greeks agreed to leave and head back to their homeland, promising to leave behind a prize for the victors. With the help of the Gods and a visit to Home Depot, it took only two days for the Greeks to build the legendary wooden horse. A handful of Greeks led by Odysseus hid inside it, while the rest of the Greeks took to their ships and hid in a nearby cove. Imagine the surprise of the Trojans to wake up one morning and find the Greeks gone and a giant model of a beautiful ebony Swedish Warmblood outside the city gates. (Of course it was a Swedish Warmblood—what type of horse did you think it was going to be?). It stood 160 hands high, with marvelous conformation, magnificent pasterns, beautiful withers, a perky poll and a really cool croup. If you do not know the meaning of these terms, please read the article entitled "Know Your Horse's Anatomy." Not now—later, when you've finished this one.

The Trojans, drunk with victory and excitement and, well, just drunk, pulled the horse into the city, despite the objections of Cassandra, the King of Troy's daughter. She pleaded with them to leave the horse outside, citing the fact that it had no Coggins, and that if you put your ear close up against it you could hear giggling. To no avail. The horse was brought in through the gates, and the drunken Trojans fell asleep, leaving the horse unguarded. You all know what happened next—the Greek warriors inside the horse all died of asphyxiation because they had forgotten to drill air holes in its side. No, that's not true, the Greeks came out of the hidden trap door and opened the gates of the city, allowing the Greek army to come charging in and, basically, massacre everyone. A terrible fate for the poor Trojans but, frankly, they must have been pretty dumb to bring the horse into the city in the first place—not the sort of people that you would want in your gene pool. The jubilant Greeks set off for home, but the gods were so angry at the Greek savagery that they allowed very few of them to survive the journey.

So, in a nutshell, that's the story of the first dressage competition. You might wonder why Homer in the *Iliad* and Virgil in *Dressage Today* failed to mention the dressage competition in their recounting of the story of the Trojan Horse. Me too. But one can't argue with the veracity of ancient scrolls, now, can one? So, next time one of those thoroughbred owners boasts that horse racing is the sport of kings, you can politely inform her, "That might well be so, but dressage is the sport of the gods."

Classified Ads
What you need, going cheap

Ribbons, Medals, Plaques, quality reproductions for sale. Includes any inscription at no charge. We defy anyone to tell the difference from the real thing. Be the envy of everyone at your barn, impress your friends and colleagues. Avoid the stress and expense of actually competing. USDF Gold medals a specialty. Send for free catalog. CindyLou@fitchburgstateprison.org.

Good Home Wanted for male companion, 53 year old Software Designer. All shots, clicker trained, some arthritis, slight odor. A bit past it, if you get my drift. Call Celia at 713-552-8731.

For Sale, Magnificent 25 acre dressage property in the Hamptons. 5 year old contemporary mansion, 8 bdrms, 12,500 sq., ft, 6 car garage, gunite pool, tennis court. Beautiful 12 stall barn, full size indoor arena with private viewing area, 2 outdoor rings, 15 large paddocks, various outbuildings, separate manager's cottage. Offered at $21.8m. Or will swap for a Grand Prix score over 65 just once. Contact DeluxRealty@willbribe.com

Achin' in Aachen? Age 25, single, straight, female dressage rider, blond, attractive, slim but with appealing figure seeks middle-aged European trainer in need of U.S. green card. Will wed sight unseen if you fit the profile. Must be certified to FEI level training. Prefer German, Dutch or Danish. Owning own Grand Prix horse a definite plus. Breeding a possibility. Send resume, plus photo of horse to: Debbie@ALO.com

Equine Spray Paint. Tired of the same old horse? Spruce up the beast with our harmless, non-toxic horse paints. Used in Hollywood westerns. Turn a roan into a grey, a bay into a palomino, a paint into another paint in less than 30 mins. Takes about 1 gal. for average horse. Washes off with water. Blaze dyes also available. Call Carlos at 203-562-1171.

Will Swap Italian boyfriend, almost handsome, well-mannered, a bit dim, for really good saddle. Call Mary 617-991-4242.

Earn Extra Money on your weekends. American Civil War re-enactment society desperately needs cavalry. If you own a horse and are interested in history then come join the fun and refight the battles of Manassas, Fredricksburg, Chancellorsville and Spotsylvania. Uniform, rifle and saber will be provided. Pick your side—Reb or Fed. Horse must be calm and disciplined around drums, bugles, cannon fire and mass musketry fire. You must be prepared to ride all day in sweltering southern Virginia summer wearing heavy serge uniform. Contact: BobbieLee@appomattox.net

Horse Pajamas made to order. Tops and bottoms, made of lightweight fleece. Keep your horse warm on winter nights and fly-free in summer, be the envy of your barn. Pink for mares, blue for stallions. Plus monogram service available. Call Lisa at 981-189-9810.

Used Dressage Video Games for your PlayStation or Xbox at a fraction (nine tenths) of their original price. Choose Olympic 2000 and World Cup editions. Compete against the world's best horses and riders. Thrill to the polite applause from the crowd and the accolades from the judges. Mount the victory stand and ride the victory gallop! Also available, for the video game expert, the extremely challenging "Parking a Goose-Neck Trailer" game. Rush $19.95 (plus $49.95 P&H) to Secondhand Sally Inc. N.Y. N.Y. 01202.

Dressage Vacation Adventures. Don't waste your precious vacation time on those dreary equine holiday packages, like trailing through the Loire Valley or trotting the Great Wall of China. Take the next step up to our exclusive dressage rider's action adventures. Try two weeks touring with the **Royal Canadian Mounted Police** demonstration team. Don the scarlet jacket and Mounties hat as you quadrille your way across North America. Take part in the famous "cantering through the ranks with lances down" movement. (Full medical insurance essential). Or thrill to the excitement as a member of Argentina's crack **Mounted Riot Control**

Squad as they break up political demonstrations in Buenos Aires. Feel the exhilaration of the crack of the baton on skulls and the crushing of bones under hooves. Our special this month is to become a temporary member of the fabulous **Spanish Riding School of Vienna**. Learn how to perform the Capriole and Croupade movements, be treated with utter contempt by the Austrian riders, and maybe show those Lipizzans the meaning of the word 'extension'. Send for free brochure to: Maggie@madcap.com

Free Manure: Come and get it. 2 to 3 years old. Add zing to your zucchini, tang to your tomatoes, crunch to your carrots. Pure, organic, New England special warmblood manure only—no additives. Will help load. Stop by in Harvard MA, have a glass of Chablis, a little baked Brie, load up your truck and I will gladly sign this book for you. Brian McKeown.